DESPERADO

IN RECKLESS PURSUIT OF A RELENTLESS JESUS

Brian's & Sara's
↳ *Pastor*
↓

Dr. David L. Clark

CENTRAL CHRISTIAN

Beloit, Wisconsin

9/17

DESPERADO: In Reckless Pursuit of a Relentless Jesus
CENTRAL CHRISTIAN publishing
Central Christian Church
2460 Milwaukee Road
Beloit, WI 53511
www.centralwired.com

Copy Editor: Robin Benskin
Designer: Amanda Urish
Photography: A special thank you to the talented Ben White for the use of his photography provided through *unsplash.com* (A website devoted to providing "high-resolution photos ... by the world's most generous community of photographers.")

Desperado/Dr. David L. Clark —1st ed.
ISBN 978-0-692-92626-0

DEDICATION

Hoping every word is an honor to the ONE AND ONLY, whose Name is above all names, our relentless Jesus, the Divine Desperado.

To Central Christian, a church full of desperados, committed to bring, belong, serve and grow in the glorious likeness of the Lord of Life.

To my parents, Bill and Nadine Clark, who were my first examples of the desperado life.

Contents

[VI] *Desperados*

DESPERADO

How to Use this Book

A RECKLESS PURSUIT of Jesus is not a sprint. It's more a marathon. Jesus warned that He would have followers who would spring up fast and die off just as fast. The desperado life is an endurance contest. Desperados know the promise of James, the brother of our Lord: "Anyone who meets a testing challenge head-on and manages to stick it out is mighty fortunate. For such a person, loyally in love with God, the reward is life and more life." (James 1:12 MSG)

Pray right now for endurance to do the next forty days in reckless pursuit of Jesus.

My first book, *"I AM" Crazy*, was also a forty day spiritual adventure of listening and learning from the great "I AM". It was a call for people interested in Jesus, intrigued by Jesus, to discover who He said He is and what He longs to do in and for our lives.

This desperado book is a follow-up to the first. I want people to experience more of Jesus. I am deeply troubled by what I see in most churches across our nation today. The average congregation in the U.S. has less than 100 people. 85% of American churches are at best stagnant and at worst in disappointing decline. Could it be that there are simply too many church-goers and not enough Christ-followers?

As believers, we certainly talk a good deal about following Jesus. But at times it feels like the phrase has lost its meaning. It's a cliche that needs to be resurrected from the dead. That's exactly what I want to see happen in your life over the next 40 days.

Jesus has made us the target of His relentless love, His relentless mercy, His relentless protection and provision. Jesus prays for us relentlessly. Jesus relentlessly works all things to our good. Jesus relentlessly sustains and strengthens. I want to know what it means to truly follow Jesus. I believe Jesus is the Way, the Truth and the Life. So, I want to make my life all about following Him. I believe Jesus is Lord of lords and King of kings. I'm desperate to do whatever it takes to follow Him. This book is an invitation for you to join me in reckless pursuit of Jesus.

Two things you need to know about Jesus up front: 1) It was His habit to be in worship every weekend; 2) He did His spiritual journey with a small group of friends. So, make a heartfelt commitment now to practice three spiritual disciplines for the next six weeks.

Read a portion of this book each day. Be present and engaged in worship at church every weekend. And join a small group of desperados in reckless pursuit of Jesus

At the end of each day's reading is **The Desperado Daily.** You will find a portion of God-breathed Scripture to ponder throughout the day; a spiritual action to put into practice that day and a prayer to serve as a conversation-starter between you and your Lord.

Obviously, this book is not an exhaustive work on what it means to follow Jesus. I felt the Spirit leading me to focus on unique passages in Luke's record of the life, ministry, death and resurrection of Jesus. Luke includes stories, miracles and prayers of Jesus that do not appear in the books by Matthew, Mark and John. These special scenes with the spotlight on Jesus — leading and loving, teaching and touching, making prayers and making promises — will set the stage for our joyous journey.

Let's get ready to get reckless. We have a relentless Jesus to pursue with all our heart.

DESPERADO

DAY 1

The Truth We Can Handle

"YOU CAN'T HANDLE THE TRUTH!" Arrogant anger gave birth to these sobering words. Col. Jessup, played by Jack Nicholson, coldly spat them out in the military courtroom drama, "A Few Good Men." *"You can't handle the truth!"*

Social science seems to agree with Col. Jessup. Evidently, we all have difficulty dealing with the truth, particularly when it gets personal. Most people cannot handle the truth about themselves. Most people will make every effort to put out of their head any facts that make them look bad. They refuse to deal with any evidence indicating they are way-off in their thinking, that they are a bad person, or that there might be something very wrong with them. Most people only accept and believe information that confirms that they are a good person, holding right opinions and preferences.

In psychology, this is called "confirmation bias." We confirm our bias toward ourselves. We accept what makes us look good. We don't believe anything that makes us look bad. I have this tendency in me. You have this tendency in you. We all have a hard time handling the hard truth about ourselves.

But there is something even more disturbing about each of us. We all tend to do what psychology calls "identity-protective thinking."

Here's how this works. Remember, we already have this confirmation bias, believing whatever makes us look good and disbelieving anything that makes us look bad. If you and I have a disagreement, we protect our personal identities by attacking each other. I am right, so you must be wrong. I know I'm a good person. You must be bad. In fact, I will protect my identity at all costs, even to the point of making you out to be evil.

But demonizing the other person is not enough for us. We go to friends and family to tell them how awful this other person is. "Can you believe what they said to me?" "Can you believe what they did to me?" In order to protect the way we want others to think of us, we poison their thinking about the person with whom we have the conflict.

We all can have a hard time handling the truth about ourselves, which can cause us to think ugly thoughts, hold bitter feelings, say and do hateful things.

I've told you all this because I want to take a big risk up front. I need to tell you the truth about me. Here's the first thing you should know: I have a sick heart. My heart disease is not physical, but spiritual. My sick heart deceives me into loving things more than people. It deceives me into thinking my emotions are telling me the truth. My sick heart gets filled with longings, driven by wrong desires. Ugh. It's not a pretty picture. I'm just being real about myself. Though what is true of my heart is also true of yours.

The Maker of all human hearts puts it this way:

"The heart is deceitful above all things and beyond cure." (Jeremiah 17:9 NIV)

When Jeremiah wrote this truth, the Hebrew phrase he used for "beyond cure" could be translated "desperately sick". That's the honest truth about your heart and mine.

As long as I'm being honest, I might as well tell more of the truth. I also have a dark mind. I can think dark thoughts. Sometimes my thoughts are dark toward myself and I get discouraged and disappointed. Sometimes my thoughts are dark toward others and I get angry and bitter. Other times my thoughts get dark toward the future, making me worried and afraid. The worst times are when my thoughts get dark toward God, which kills my hope.

According to the Bible, I'm not the only one.

"For although they knew God they did not honor Him as God or give thanks to Him, but they became petty in their thinking and their senseless minds were darkened." (Romans 1:21 RSV)

Here's the really bad news for me: If I stay dark-hearted and dark-minded, my soul goes dark. When that happens, I feel totally unworthy of God. It's a bad place to be.

That's the truth about me; but it's only half of the truth. Half the truth is a lie. Here's the whole truth. What I've told you is real; what I am going to tell you is outrageous. Jesus is not put off by the ugliness of my heart.

He loves me relentlessly. He keeps loving me, until my heart goes from ugly to beautiful. He loves the ugly right out of my heart.

There's more. Jesus is not grossed out by my dark thoughts. He loves me relentlessly. He keeps loving me, until my thinking finds a faith focus. He keeps loving me and loving me, until I function with the mind of Christ.

When my soul goes dark, Jesus does not go into gag reflex. He goes into action. He will not leave me feeling undeserving and unworthy. He restores my soul with His relentless love.

This is the confirmation bias we can believe about our relentless Jesus. We can be anchored — heart, mind and soul — to His promise. *"Jesus said to the people who believed in Him, 'You are truly My disciples if you remain faithful to My teachings.* **You will know the truth and the truth will set you free!***'"* (John 8:32 NLT)

Here's confirmation that Jesus is relentlessly biased toward us. *"God demonstrated His own love for us in this: While we were still sinners, Christ died for us."* (Romans 5:8 NIV)

We don't have to go through life always fighting to defend who we are. Our true identity is perpetually protected by the greatest power on the planet. *"How great is the love the Father has lavished on us, that we should be called children of God! And that is what we are!"* (I John 3:1 NIV)

That's the truth I can handle. Thank God! That's the truth that handles me!

THE DESPERADO DAILY

Ponder:

> "How great is the love the Father has lavished on us, that
> we should be called children of God! And that is what we
> are!" (I John 3:1 NIV)

Practice:

> Commit yourself now to make your pursuit of Jesus
> the most important action in your day every day. Get
> desperate for His relentless love.

Pray:

> "Dear Lord Jesus, thank You for Your relentless love.
> Thank You for never giving up on me no matter how
> dark and damaged I can be. Lord, thank You for Your
> Word that teaches me the truth about myself, as a child
> of the Father. You free my heart to be healed of hurtful
> emotions. You free my mind to be filled with thoughts
> of You. You free my very soul with an understanding
> of how deeply valued I am by You. I am desperate for
> You. I am in passionate pursuit of more of You. In Your
> Name, Amen!"

DESPERADO

DAY 2

God Chose the Despised

WHEN YOU THINK "relentless", think this series of synonyms: constant, continual, never-ending, persistent, unceasing, unstoppable, non-stop, endless.

When you think of Jesus, think of His relentless work to our good — constant protection, continual provision, never-ending hope, persistent prayer, unceasing peace, non-stop loving kindness, compassion, mercy and grace, unstoppable power. All these qualities are varied reflections of His endless love.

What the relentless, endless love of Jesus does for us at the deepest levels came at the highest cost to Himself. Jesus couldn't fix all that is dark and broken within us by giving us a self-help book or putting us in a 12-step group or offering us a series of counseling sessions.

There was only one way for Jesus to root out what is desperately sick within us. To get us free of our diseased selves, Jesus took upon Himself all of our sin sickness.

He was literally made to be our sin. *"God made Him who had no sin to be sin for us, so that in Him we could be put right with God."* (II Corinthians 5:21 NIV, MSG)

On the surface this looks so unfair. Jesus knew no sin and did no sin. Yet He took on Himself our sin sickness. Why? He did it FOR us. His love FOR us was so relentless, that He would not be put off by what was so ugly and most offensive about us.

How did this work? When Paul explained it by writing, *"God made Him...to be sin"*, his audience likely would have read, *"God made Him...to be a sin offering."*

This is a picture of Christ dying on the cross in our place to pay for our sin. Talk about relentless love. On the cross Jesus was your substitute. He took the punishment you deserved for your sin. Jesus died the hellish death I should die for my sin. All God's anger due me fell on Jesus. All God's condemnation due you fell on Jesus. All God's judgment rightly due us for our sin fell on Jesus. A sinless Savior was our sin offering.

By Jesus' death on the cross in my place and the fact that three days later He rose from the dead, now I can be justified — "just-as-if-I" never sinned. Isn't that wild?

In fact, here's what the Bible says: it is possible for me to be *"justified in the name of the Lord Jesus Christ."* (I Corinthians 6:11 NIV) — just-as-if-I never sinned.

I know how sinfully deceitful my emotions can be. I know how sinfully dark my mind can be. I know I deserve hell. There is nothing I want more than to be in relationship with Jesus, so that it's just as if I never sinned. There is nothing I want more for you right now than for it to be just as if you never sinned. How is that possible?

Jesus doesn't leave us in the dark on this one. He tells a creative story on how we can be justified. We find

Jesus telling this story in the book of Luke 18:9-14. But He sets up the story in the opening line of Luke 18. *"Jesus told them a story, showing that it was necessary for them to pray..."* (Luke 18:1)

There is a way to pray that will get us justified before God — just as if we never sinned.

The New International Version of the New Testament uses just two words in Luke 18:9 to set the scene for why Jesus tells this compelling story — *"To some..."* The Greek words for "to some" are "tivas tous". I love what they actually mean. We might say it this way: "To anybody and everybody."

Jesus relentlessly loves anybody and everybody. Jesus, though fully God, became fully human for anybody and everybody. Jesus tenaciously and triumphantly overcame all temptation to live a sinless life for anybody and everybody. Jesus died for anybody and everybody. God raised Jesus from the dead for anybody and everybody — every kind of person, every color of person, every culture of person. It is the heart of Jesus to provide justification from sin for anybody and everybody.

It's just that some of the anybodies in Jesus' audience think they are big somebodies and everyone else is a bunch of nobodies. The Revised Standard Version of the New Testament gives us an important insight. *"He also told this story to those who trusted in themselves that they were right with God and who despised others."* (Luke 18:9)

Jesus is aiming His story at those who think they are good enough for God and everyone else is good for nothing. In fact, the Greek word originally used in this text for "despised" is "exoutheneo." It is formed by combining two Greek words: "ek" (from) and "ouden" (nothing).

These holier-than-thou snobs would look down their noses at everyone else and say, "You're nothing. You've got nothing. You're a nobody from nowhere." In the day of Jesus, this was the worst possible thing you could say about anybody.

It's interesting to me that this same Greek word for "despised" appears two other times in the Bible. In Luke 23, this is what Herod's soldiers are saying to Jesus on the day of his death, "You're nothing. You've got nothing. You're nobody from nowhere. You're dead meat."

What's most exciting to me is that this same word appears in I Corinthians 1:28 — *"God chose...the despised."* God chooses people who are nothing, who have nothing, nobodies, from nowhere. I love the fact that nobodies are God's first choice.

A good English word for "ek ouden" might be desperado. We tend to think a desperado is someone outside the law. But originally, the word meant a nobody with nothing, desperate enough to take reckless action to get something of substance for their life.

As I did these word studies, something went off in my heart. I decided I wanted to be a desperado for Jesus. I decided to write this book as an invitation for others to join me in being **Desperados, in reckless pursuit of a relentless Jesus!**

If my Jesus sided with the "ek ouden", if Jesus Himself was considered "ek ouden", if my God makes the "ek ouden" His first choice, then I will be a spiritual desperado in reckless pursuit of my relentless Jesus. If you're willing to join me, keep reading. Jesus has a "desperado" story for you.

THE DESPERADO DAILY

Ponder:

"Isn't it obvious that God deliberately chose men and women that the culture overlooks and exploits and abuses, chose these "nobodies" to expose the hollow pretensions of the "somebodies"? That makes it quite clear that none of you can get by with blowing your own horn before God. Everything that we have — right thinking and right living, a clean slate and a fresh start — comes from God by way of Jesus Christ." (I Corinthians 1:28-30 MSG)

Practice:

Think of Jesus' relentless loving work to our good — constant protection, continual provision, never-ending hope, persistent prayer, unceasing peace, non-stop loving kindness, compassion, mercy, grace and His unstoppable power.

Pray:

"Dear Lord, thank You for choosing me. Please, help me keep choosing You, passionately pursuing Your relentless love. I love You! In Your precious Name, Amen!"

DESPERADO

DAY 3

Humility:
Where Heaven
Draws Near

"TWO MEN WENT *up to the temple to pray, one a Pharisee and the other a tax collector. The tax collector stood up and prayed about himself: 'God, I thank You that I am not like other men — robbers, evildoers, adulterers — or even like this tax collector. I fast twice a week and give a tenth of all I get.' But the tax collector stood at a distance. He would not even look up to heaven, but beat his breast and said, 'God, have mercy on me, a sinner.' I tell you that this man, rather than the other, went home justified before God. For everyone who exalts himself will be humbled, and he who humbles himself will be exalted!"* (Luke 18:10-14 NIV)

This is the story Jesus told, so you can know how to be justified before God, just as if you never sinned. This is how a desperado begins to recklessly follow Jesus.

Let's go over the story piece by piece, starting with the two main characters. *"Two men went up to the temple to pray, one a Pharisee and the other a tax collector."* (Luke 18:10)

A Pharisee is a holier-than-thou person who thinks he's better than everybody else. In the story, the tax collector is the "ek ouden" — the nobody with nothing from nowhere.

"The Pharisee stood up and prayed about himself" (Luke 18:11 NIV). This could easily be translated, "he prayed to himself." Either way, about himself or to himself, this guy thinks that he is all good with God. But God doesn't even hear his prayer.

He prays like this. *"God, I thank you that I am not like other men, robbers, evildoers, adulterers, or even like this tax collector. I fast twice a week and give a tenth of all I get."* (Luke 18:12 NIV)

This really religious guy puts himself on center stage, pats himself on the back, making a public announcement to one and all how awesome he is. It's supposed to be a time of prayer, but he's made the moment all about himself. That's the very opposite of a desperado.

Here's the picture Jesus paints of someone in reckless pursuit of His relentless love. *"But the tax collector stood at a distance."* (Luke 18:13 NIV)

This tax collector knows he deserves nothing from God. He doesn't force his way to center stage. He stays on the fringe. Maybe he only comes one step inside the temple, feeling that's all he deserves from God. He sees himself as spiritually bankrupt, in desperate need of God.

See how Jesus describes him. *"He would not even look up to heaven."* (Luke 18:13)

Ironically, this is the kind of humility that actually gains heaven. In His Sermon on the Mount, Jesus said it this way, *"Blessed are the poor in spirit, for theirs is the kingdom of Heaven."* (Matthew 5:3 NIV)

There are those so aware of their spiritual nothingness they can't even lift their head. They just raise their hands and beg. They know they are totally dependent on God.

This guy is such a desperate desperado *"he beat his breast."* (Luke 18:13 NIV)

In that culture, men would never beat their breast. Women would, if they were grieving. On the rare, rare occasion when a man would beat his breast, he did so as a sign that he was desperate for God, recklessly pursuing God as his only hope.

Do you know another huge moment, when this image of chest-beating appears in the Bible? At the death of Jesus, *"When all the people who had gathered to witness this sight saw what took place, they beat their breasts and went away."* (Luke 23:48 NIV)

In that day men only beat their chests as a sign they were trying to beat the evil out of their hearts. This man humbly has his head down. He beats his chest to show that he accepts the hard truth about himself. He has a sick heart. He has a dark mind. His soul is in desperate need of God. He then cries out this prayer:

"God, have mercy on me, a sinner." (Luke 18:13 NIV)

Asking for mercy is asking God to show His love and kindness. Asking for mercy is asking for God to protect us from the consequences we deserve for our sin. Asking for mercy is acknowledging that we can't save ourselves and that we desperately need God. Asking for mercy is a reckless prayer that God answers every time.

The humble will be honored

We can trust this to be true, because this is how Jesus climaxes His story. *"I tell you that this man, rather than the other, went home justified before God."* (Luke 18:14 NIV)

This man goes home justified before God, just as if he had never sinned. This can happen to you. You are just one prayer away from being justified before God, just as if you never sinned.

I have decided that this is what I want for my life. I want to be a desperado for Jesus. So I am making this desperado prayer, my prayer. "Lord have mercy on me, a sinner."

Do you know the cool thing about being a desperado and knowing the truth about yourself — that you're nothing, a nobody from nowhere? It's the final thing Jesus said. It's His promise: *"Everyone...who humbles himself will be exalted."* (Luke 18:14 NIV)

This means the humble are personally exalted by God Himself. I want to experience a God-exalted life with a God-exalted heart, a God-exalted mind, a God-exalted soul. Thus, I'm a desperado, inviting you to be a desperado, recklessly pursuing a relentless Jesus.

Lord have mercy on me.

THE DESPERADO DAILY

Ponder:

"Blessed are the poor in spirit, for theirs is the Kingdom of heaven." (Matthew 5:3 NIV)

Practice:

Humble yourself before the Lord.

Pray:

"God, have mercy on me, a sinner! In the mighty Name of Jesus, Amen!"

Yes, Lord have mercy on me.

DESPERADO

DAY 4

God, Have Mercy on Me, a Sinner

MY FRIEND WAS having a proverbial dark night of the soul. His wife was gone on a business trip. He was alone, sitting on the floor in the middle of their bedroom. He had turned off the lights. But he couldn't bring himself to crawl into bed alone. He dreaded the very thought of waking up to another empty, empty day.

He hated what his life had become. On the outside, everything looked good — good wife, good friends, good job, good times. It was just that the good times were feeling very bad — unbearably bad. He drank and partied to keep the bad feeling at bay. It wasn't working. What was wrong with him?

On the inside he was coming painfully apart at the seams. He wanted a drink right then in the worst way. But he knew his drinking had become his personal poison — hurting himself, harming those he cared about most, killing any hint of hope. His life was going down the wrong path. His life was going to hell.

He began to weep. As he did, something came over him. My friend would later say, "Some supernatural Someone came over him." He knelt in the dark and began to call on the Lord, "If You are real, if You are there, I need You. I need help."

All these years later I'm not sure exactly what else he included in his prayer. But I think our Heavenly Father heard it like this: "God, have mercy on me, a sinner!"

My friend got up off his knees a new man. He and his wife began to attend our church. The night the Light washed over his dark soul, I would say he became a desperado for Jesus. All these decades later he is still in reckless pursuit of our relentless Lord.

What did being a desperado for Jesus look like for my friend? He was committed to being in worship every weekend possible. He refused to be like the average church-goer in the U.S. who's only in worship once a month. He believed that if God is real and He is there for us, He is worthy of committed worship. For my friend, being a desperado for Jesus was a life-style — to be regularly in God's Word, to be recklessly generous in his giving, to be a reliable volunteer, serving others as God had served him.

Just like my friend, your desperado adventure can begin with that simple, humble cry of the heart, "God, have mercy on me, a sinner." When you pray that prayer, the same thing will happen to you that happened to my friend. You get justified before God. It's just as if you never sinned. The first step in following Jesus is a reckless prayer.

The second step in following Jesus is also a prayer. But it's not you praying. It's Jesus praying for you. Isn't that a wild thought? If you are a desperado, Jesus, the Lord of all creation, is praying for you. In fact, the number one thing on His to-do list today is to pray for you. *"Jesus is able to save completely those who come to God through Him because He always lives to pray for them."* (Hebrews 7:25)

This is one of the big benefits of being a desperado for Jesus. When you begin to recklessly pursue Him, He prays relentlessly for you. Can you imagine this? Jesus is at the right hand of God. When He sees you pursuing Him in worship, in His Word, with your generosity, and by serving others, Jesus leans over to the Father's ear and begins to tell God everything you need. There is no one who has more influence with the Father in your behalf than Jesus the Son.

Here's the glorious good news for all desperados:

When we pursue Jesus recklessly, He prays for us relentlessly.

Remember that series of synonyms for "relentless" — constant, continual, never-ending, persistent, unceasing, unstoppable, non-stop, endless. Now meditate a moment on how each of these words accurately portrays the prayer work of Jesus in your behalf. Doesn't that just blow your mind?

Jesus constantly prays that you will be a desperado. He prays continually for you to recklessly pursue Him. Jesus has a never-ending supply of prayers, marked with your name. When you forget to pray, He persists in praying for you. Jesus tirelessly brings your concerns before the Father. His prayers for you are non-stop and unceasing. Satan may stop us from praying. But the prayers of Jesus are unstoppable. As we actively pursue Him, the prayers of Jesus in our behalf are without end. Wow!

I love the painting that depicts Jesus lovingly praying over a child who is at rest in bed. But there is always more to our Jesus than what can be captured in one picture. In reality, Jesus is ever lovingly in prayer over all of His followers, both young and old. He does pray over us as we sleep. But Jesus also covers our every waking hour.

Maybe you ask, "How is that possible?" Here's how: Jesus is the unlimited Lord of lords. He is at a position of all-authority at the very right hand of the Father. Our Jesus has infinite focus on all His desperados, who are in reckless pursuit of His relentless love.

Consider this exciting example from John 17 of how I believe Jesus might pray for us:

> *"Father...You granted (Me) authority over all people that (I) might give eternal life to all those You have given (Me)...that they may know You, the only true God and Jesus Christ whom You have sent...I pray for them. I am not praying for the world, but for those You have given Me, for they are Yours...Holy Father, protect them by the power of Your Name, the Name You gave Me, so they may be one as We are one...that they may have the full measure of My joy within them...My prayer is not that you take them out of the world, but that You protect them from the evil one...Father, I want those You have given Me to be with Me where I am, and to see My glory..." (John 17:2,3,9,11,13,15,24 NIV)*

We should not be surprised that following Jesus, as spiritual desperados, begins with prayer. We pursue Him recklessly with the humble prayer, "God, have mercy on me, a sinner." He loves us relentlessly, always keeping us as the focus of His faithful prayers.

THE DESPERADO DAILY

Ponder:

When we pursue Jesus recklessly, He prays for us relentlessly.

Practice:

Make being a desperado for Jesus a life-style. Commit yourself to be in His worship each weekend, to be in His Word each day, to find a place of service in His church; to share your faith with others; and to give as generously as possible.

Pray:

"Lord Jesus, I am sorry for all the times I forget to pray. Thank You for praying for me. Thank You for continually calling the Father's attention to my needs and concerns. Please help me grow in my relationship with You. I love you. In Your Name. Amen."

[24] *Desperado*

DESPERADO
DAY 5

The Prayer Work of Jesus

ON MY BEST day, I'm not a very good person. I get one area of my life right, then get another wrong. I keep my mouth shut when I'm tempted to say something bad. Then I catch myself thinking something terrible. Dang it. With all my perfectionistic efforts to keep everything on the up-and-up, I always find some way to fall, flop or fail — publicly or privately, as a pastor or a parent, with my family or with a friend. But my very worst moments are my sins against a holy God, who has never been anything but good to me.

Unfortunately for you, the truth is: we are much alike. *"We're all sin-infected, sin-contaminated. Our best efforts are grease-stained rags."* (Isaiah 64:6 MSG)

King David could barely bear his "rags" reality. Feel the cry of his heart to God:

> *"Blot out the stain of my sins. Wash me clean from my guilt. Purify me from my sin. I recognize my rebellion.*

It haunts me day and night. Against You and You alone, have I sinned. I have done what is evil in Your sight." (Psalm 51:1-4 NLT)

Another Bible biggie, the Apostle Paul, shows gut-level frustration, when he writes:

"I don't really understand myself, for I want to do what is right, but I don't do it. Instead I do what I hate." (Romans 7:15 NLT)

At the end of the same chapter Paul puts on a mini-Q&A session for all who wrestle with sin's inner anguish. *"What a miserable person I am! Who can free me from this life that is dominated by sin and death? Thank God! The answer is Jesus Christ our Lord!"* (Romans 7:24,25 NLT)

How is Jesus our ultimate answer? Paul tells us at the end of the very next chapter. *"Christ Jesus, who died — more than that, who was raised to life — is at the right hand of God and is also interceding (praying) for us."* (Romans 8:34 NIV)

I love the way John, the best friend of Jesus, celebrates the prayer work of Jesus in our behalf. *"If you sin, there is Someone to plead (pray) for you before the Father. His name is Jesus Christ, the One who is all that is good and who pleases God completely."* (I John 2:1 LB)

To show you how incredibly important this is, let me take you into a Jesus story. This story took place very late on the night before Jesus was crucified. He knew that within 24 hours He would be dead.

Jesus hosts a simple, intimate dinner party for twelve of His closest friends. At the climax of the evening, He takes a loaf of bread, thanks God for it, breaks it and passes it around to His friends and says, "This bread is My body, broken for you. Eat it and remember My sacrifice."

In the same way, He takes a cup of wine, thanks God for it and says, "This is My blood, poured out for the forgiveness of your sins. Drink from it, all of you. Do this and remember My sacrificial death."

2,000 years later desperados still take Jesus at His Word. Every weekend, as we worship, we remember His death, just as our Lord commanded us. We call it the Lord's Supper. We eat a bit of bread and drink a sip of grape juice, grateful that He died so our sins could be forgiven; our hearts cleansed of all guilt and shame. I believe every week Jesus prays that you'll be in worship on the weekend to remember His death for you.

But Jesus was not done with His friends. He had more for them, just as He has more for you right now, as you read. This is a deeply personal moment. Jesus turns to the person on His right. When He does, all table conversation stops.

Jesus' full focus is solely now on Peter. Actually His name is Simon. Simon was the name his parents had given him. Jesus nicknamed him Peter, which means "the rock".

But let's take careful notice of how Jesus addresses Peter now. It has the same feel for how Jesus addresses us. *"Simon, Simon..."* (Luke 22:31 NIV)

By using his name twice, Jesus is saying, "Simon, this is serious. Simon, I want your full attention," which just happened to get the full attention of every man around the table. And that's a good thing, because Jesus was talking about every man around the table. In fact, his talk includes us as well. This is what he said,

"Simon, Simon, Satan has asked to sift you as wheat."
(Luke 22:31 NIV)

This is not your normal level of dinner conversation. Jesus does not have time to mess around. He knows that by 9:00 the next morning He'll be spiked to a blood-stained cross. This is like Jesus giving Simon a spiritual warning shot — Simon, Simon.

Jesus is confrontational, because He is concerned. Jesus is confrontational, because He can make a difference, when Peter does the worst thing at the worst time. Jesus confronts Peter just as He confronts us, announcing to us all that we have an evil enemy. In fact, the name Satan means adversary.

Jesus wants Simon and us never to forget that Satan is out to destroy us. When Jesus described Satan, He called him a thief who comes after us, seeking to steal, kill, and destroy (John 10:10). That's the bad news. Satan is all about our death.

The good news is Jesus is all about our life. He promised in the same breath, *"I have come that they might have life and have it to the full."* (John 10:10 NIV)

We may never be comfortable with not being good enough. But we can surely worship a Savior who is absolutely good and who is relentlessly good to those who pursue Him with reckless abandon. We will always need His mercy and He'll always give it in great abundance. Maybe more important than our prayers to Him are His prayers for us. By His prayers we win over the evil one. By His prayers we are unconditionally accepted by a glorious God. By His prayers we receive peace, strength, joy, love, hope — all we need for a good life. Maybe we should pray gratefully that Jesus always prays for us.

THE DESPERADO DAILY

Ponder:

Satan, our adversary, is a liar, thief and murderer, who is out to destroy us.

Practice:

Worship the Savior who is absolutely good and who is relentlessly good to those who pursue Him with reckless abandon.

Pray:

"Lord Jesus, You are majestic and amazing. I am too often a mess. I am grateful for all your prayer work in my behalf. You pray for me and I find strength; I find peace; I find the Father's favor. Thank You, Lord, for all Your prayers. In Your Name, Amen."

His Incomparably Great Power

"DAVID, DAVID, SATAN has asked to sift you as wheat."

To be honest, if Christ Himself came to me with such a warning, including Satan and myself in the same sentence, it would shake me to the core, frighten me senseless.

What is wrong with me that my initial instinct is always fear?

When it happens to Simon, he doesn't seem to be afraid. But maybe he's just blowing smoke, when he brags: "*Lord, I'm ready to go with You to prison and to death?*"

How easily we forget that whatever Jesus does is always driven by His relentless love.

When He gets real with us, it's not to scare us. He is not looking for a false sense of bravado. When Jesus allows us to know what's coming, it's actually a trust test.

Jesus is looking for our confidence that, as God, He knows everything that's going to happen before it happens. This is the message he wants seared on Simon's soul. It's His hope for me and anyone else who desires to be a desperado for Jesus.

Here's how He said it in the book of Revelation:

> *"Do not be afraid. I am the First and the Last. I am the Living One. I was dead, and behold I am alive forever and ever. And I hold the keys of death and hell."* (Revelation 1:17-18 NIV)

This is our great confidence. We have an evil enemy at work against us, but Jesus sees everything Satan tries to do before he does it. Before Satan can make a move on us, Jesus is praying for us. This is the truth Jesus wants every desperado to get.

He looks Simon in the eye:

> *"Simon, Simon, Satan has asked to sift you as wheat. But I have prayed for you, Simon, that your faith may not fail."* (Luke 22:31,32 NIV)

Something jumps out at me here. Satan must ask permission before he can make any kind of move against our lives. In fact, the Greek word in the text means he must beg.

The big question is, why would Jesus permit anything Satan requests, even if he begs? Scholars have come up with all sorts of theories about this. But what makes the most sense to me, and seems most consistent with scripture, is this:

Jesus permits the pain that has the most potential to give us the most power.

We can understand how this works for us by seeing how it worked for Jesus. In less than 12 hours, God would permit Satan to orchestrate the crucifixion of Jesus.

God permits the ugliness of the cross to make Jesus unspeakably beautiful in His resurrection. Jesus is at His weakest on the cross. God allows that so He can give Him the supernatural strength to conquer death. God allows Jesus to be utterly humiliated on the cross so that He can exalt Him to the highest place.

This is the way it works for us. God will never let the work of the enemy stand. God allows evil only to shake us in ways that ultimately make us more beautiful, that ultimately exalt us, that ultimately make us stronger than we would ever be otherwise.

The apostle Paul describes it this way, *"This is His incomparably great power for us who believe. That power is like the working of His mighty strength, which He exerted in Christ when He raised Him from the dead and seated Him at His right hand in Heaven."* (Ephesians 1:19, 20)

Satan does not cause the bad things that happen in our lives. But Satan will use those bad things in an effort to kill our relationship with God. He does not cause the pain but he uses the pain to make us question the goodness of God. At the very same time Satan does this, God wants to use our pain to speak loudly to us of our need for Him. When we listen to Satan, the pain intensifies; we get weaker and stay stuck in the ugliness. When we listen to God, we get peace instead of pain. God becomes our strength, making everything beautiful in its time. This is the promise for all desperados.

This is why I see Jesus as the greatest desperado of all time. On the cross, He was unshakable, even when the worst happened to him. On the cross, Jesus prayed His way to victory over Satan. Do you want to know what his victory prayer was? It is the last prayer Jesus prayed before he died. He prayed it with all his might. *"Jesus called loudly, 'Father, I place my life in your hands.' Then he breathed his last."* (Luke 23:46 MSG) That's the prayer that leads every desperado to victory over any enemy attack. Jesus prayed that prayer and the next thing He knows He is risen from the dead, Lord of lords and King of kings. It's the prayer that would save Simon, when Satan tried to use the pain of the cross to destroy his faith. Satan would use the death of Christ to violently shake Simon's relationship with God.

In fact, when Jesus announced to Simon, "Satan has asked to sift you...", the word sift means to shake with great violence — to shake senseless — like a rag doll in the mouth of a pit bull. That's the bad news. Satan would use the pain to shake Simon.

The good news is that being the First and the Last, the Beginning and the End, Jesus saw all this coming. He had already prayed for Simon before Satan made his first move.

When Jesus prays relentlessly for His desperados, they come through the battle victoriously.

One side of the coin is that if we are desperados, Satan will try to shake us. Satan will try to use our pain to shake our faith in God. The other side of the coin is the good news that Jesus knows all of Satan's tricks. Jesus knows what Satan will try to do before He does it. So Jesus goes to work in our behalf, praying us to victory. In fact, Jesus wants to give us a victory so big over every painful impossibility that we have a super abundance of strength to share with others. That's what He promises Simon.

"Simon, Simon, Satan has asked to sift you as wheat. But I have prayed for you Simon, that your faith may not fail. And when you have turned back, strengthen your brothers."(Luke 22:31, 32)

This is an incredible promise. When desperados are shaken, we'll come through it. We will come through it with so much beauty, strength, and honor, we'll help others who are shaken. We will share the beauty, strength, and honor we have received from Christ.

Here's what Peter would go on to proclaim:

"When life gets really difficult, don't jump to the conclusion that God is not on the job. Instead, be glad that you're in the very thick of what Christ experienced. This is a spiritual refining process, with glory just around the corner." (1 Peter 4:12,13 MSG)

This is the next step in being a desperado. Expect to be shaken. But when you are recklessly pursuing Jesus, know He is praying for you and will carry you to victory. His relentless prayer will always leave you stronger, more beautiful and highly honored.

THE DESPERADO DAILY

....

Ponder:

> "When life gets really difficult, don't jump to the conclu-
> sion that God is not on the job. Instead, be glad that
> you're in the very think of what Christ experienced. This
> is a spiritual refining process, with glory just around the
> corner." (I Peter 4:12,13 MSG)

Practice:

> Trust that the Lord will bring you victoriously through
> any painful circumstance.

Pray:

> "Father, I place my life in Your hands. In Jesus' name,
> Amen."

DESPERADO
DAY 7

The Waters of Baptism

EVERYTHING IN MY life and everything in our church is to be all about following Jesus — nothing more, nothing less, nothing else!

Say that three times fast. Just kidding. Pray it three times slowly with all your heart.

Here's the big question: Who gets invited to follow Jesus? Do you have to be so holy or so religious or so goody-goody? Do you have to know so much of the Bible or give so much of your time or money? Or maybe you get to follow Jesus based on what you don't' do. You don't smoke or drink or chew or go with girls that do or listen to either country music or rap. Would any of that qualify you to follow Jesus?

What if the most important qualification for following Jesus is how desperate you are?

Personally, I am absolutely blown away by the "God-inspired" word used by the Apostle Paul, used by Jesus, and of Jesus, to describe someone qualified to follow Him. It is our English word, **"despised"**. The New Testament Greek term used for "despised" comes from the Greek root word, **"ekouden"** — "ek" means "from"; "ouden" means "nothing" — from nothing.

In the day of Jesus they might say to someone considered "ekouden": "You're nothing. You're nobody from nowhere. You've got nothing." In English we might equate "ekouden" with "desperado". This is someone who has nothing and is so nothing that they are willing to take reckless action to get something of substance for their life.

This is why I think Jesus was the greatest desperado of all time. The soldiers who killed Him held Jesus in such contempt that they basically said, "We despise you. You're a nobody from nowhere. You've got nothing, you are nothing. You're just a piece of meat."

The fact is this: by allowing Himself to be arrested and beaten, Jesus was taking the most reckless action possible. He was so desperate to save us, Jesus recklessly died on the cross for our sins, to make us right with God. This is Jesus' relentless love.

Paul wrote it this way:

"God put the wrong on Him who never did anything wrong, so we could be put right with God!"
(II Corinthians 5:21 MSG)

Also remember the mind-blower the apostle Paul reveals in 1 Corinthians 1:28 — the God of the universe chooses, as His own, those who know they are nothing — the "ekouden". God chooses for Himself desperados, who recklessly pursue a relentless Jesus.

Do you know the very first step Jesus says you are to take when you decide to be a desperado and follow Him with reckless abandon? Once you believe that Jesus is Lord and Savior, Jesus calls to you: *"Whoever believes and is baptized will be saved."* (Mark 16:16 NIV)

Do you know how to tell if you are ready to be baptized? It's when you know to pray, "God, have mercy on me, a sinner." Jesus says: "You pray that prayer and you go home justified — just as if you never sinned."

That's the joy of baptism. When you go all the way under the water, being buried with Jesus, your sins are washed away. It's just as if you never sinned."

This is the urging the Apostle Paul felt when he decided to become a desperado for Jesus:

"What are you waiting for? Get up and be baptized. Have your sins washed away by calling on the name of the Lord!" (Acts 22:16 NLT)

Peter seems to exude the same urgency when he lays it out for anyone who would be a desperado for Jesus:

"Change your life. Turn to God and be baptized, each of you in the name of Jesus Christ, so your sins are forgiven! Receive the gift of the Holy Spirit!" (Acts 2:38 MSG)

When desperados are baptized, it's meant to picture the baptism of our relentless Jesus!

Here's how Luke describes the exciting event. *"Jesus was baptized...and as He was praying, heaven was opened and the Holy Spirit descended on Him in bodily form like a dove. And a Voice came from heaven: 'You are My Son, whom I love. With You I am well pleased!'"* (Luke 3:21,22 NIV)

Put yourself in this picture with Jesus. If you have already been buried with Christ in baptism, you have received the Holy Spirit. God has whispered over your soul, "You are My child whom I love. With you I am well pleased."

If you've yet to be plunged into the watery grave with Jesus, the Lord has been praying for you to share this spiritual experience with Him. It is His passion that you would be fully forgiven, completely cleansed of all guilt and shame, filled to the full with the fullness of God, and absolutely assured that you could not be more pleasing to God. Soak in the promise of Jesus, "Whoever believes and is baptized will be saved."

When desperados are baptized, it's meant to be a personal participation in the baptism of our relentless Jesus!

"That's what baptism into the life of Jesus means. When we are lowered into the water, it is like the burial of Jesus; when we are raised up out of the water, it is like the resurrection of Jesus!" (Romans 6:3,4 MSG)

We all have a past. In baptism, we put our past behind us. We all have issues. In baptism, we bury our baggage. We all have our weaknesses. In baptism, God puts our lives on a whole new trajectory, sustained by His supernatural power.

Desperados passionately pursue Jesus in baptism to experience His relentless love.

"The waters of baptism do that for you, not by washing away dirt from your skin but by presenting you through Jesus' resurrection before God with a clear conscience. Jesus has the last word on everything and everyone, from angels to armies. He's standing right alongside God, and what He says goes." (I Peter 3:21,22 MSG)

THE DESPERADO DAILY

....

Ponder:

"Whoever believes and is baptized will be saved!" (Mark 16:16 NIV)

Practice:

"Change your life. Turn to God and be baptized, each of you, in the name of Jesus Christ, so your sins are forgiven. Receive the gift of the Holy Spirit." (Acts 2:38)

Pray:

"Dear Lord, I can never be perfect like You. Thank You for giving me a way to be like you by sharing fully in Your death, burial and resurrection through my baptism. Thank You for washing away my sin and giving me Your Spirit. In Your name, Amen."

DESPERADO
DAY 8

My Life
In Your Hands

NOW I'VE GOT to be straight with you. Jesus makes it clear that being a desperado will not be a walk in the park. In fact, He issues this warning:

When we follow Jesus, there will be times that Satan will attempt to shake us senseless.

Here's what we have already learned. Satan does not necessarily cause everything bad that happens in our lives. When something bad does happen, the evil one wants to use the painful problem to violently shake our trust in the goodness of God. Jesus warns us of Satan's evil intent so we will stay the course of passionately pursuing Him.

But here's the good news — Jesus will always help us stand strong no matter what kind of shaking is going on around us or within us. In fact, Jesus promised to always get us to victory. He even gives us a special prayer to help us win every time we're all shook up. This is the last prayer Jesus prayed, before He died on the cross, *"Father, I place My life in your hands!"* (Luke 23:46 MSG)

This is a prayer of total trust, letting go and letting God. This is a prayer anchored to God's promises. We know God "...is able to do immeasurably more than all we ask or imagine according to His power that is at work within us" (Ephesians 3:20) and "We know that in all things God works for the good of those who love Him, who have been called according to His purpose" (Romans 8:28). We trust with all our hearts and we pray, "Father, I place my life in your hands. I place My family and friends in Your hands. I place my finances, my feelings, even my faith in Your hands. I trust that You're good."

These are prayers everyone essentially prays when they are baptized. "God, have mercy on me, a sinner" and "Father, I place my life in your hands!" But we don't just pray these prayers when we begin to follow Jesus. The secret to winning, winning, and winning every day through every kind of shaking is to pray these prayers every day.

Let me give you a third prayer desperados pray, recklessly pursuing a relentless Jesus:

Prayer #1
"God, have mercy on me, a sinner!"

Prayer #2
"Father, I place my life in Your hands!"

Prayer #3
"Father...not my will, but Yours, be done!"
(Luke 22:42 ESV)

Let me give you the back-story for this prayer. Jesus Himself prays it very late on the night before He is crucified. By 9 o'clock the next morning Jesus will be writhing in agony, dangling helplessly from a criminal's cross — face beaten beyond recognition; lashed so severely, His back will be one, giant, bloody wound — skin torn away, muscles exposed, suffering horrific loss of blood. Spikes will be driven through His wrists and ankles into the cross. He will endure this hellish torture for six excruciating hours. By three o'clock in the afternoon Jesus will be dead. The crazy thing is this: He knows it. He knows every grotesque detail.

For the last year, over and over again, Jesus has been telling His disciples that this ugly, awful day was coming. They either never believed Him or never understood, when He said, *"We are on our way to Jerusalem. The Son of Man will be betrayed to the religious leaders. They will sentence Him to death. They will hand Him over to the Romans for mockery and torture and crucifixion. On the third day, He will be raised up alive."* (Matthew 22:18,19 MSG)

Now this dark, dire, devastating, disastrous day has come. I run out of ugly adjectives. There are not enough words to rightly describe the fierce, fiendish fury of hell on earth. To Jesus, it feels like He's being shaken with great violence by all the forces of evil.

Here's how Luke unfolds the story.

"Jesus went out..."

He's being swarmed by every demon in hell. But Jesus isn't backing out of God's plan. Evil is trying to knock Him off track, but Jesus is not backing down. He is not going on the defensive. Jesus went out on the attack. He is wading headlong into a wicked war. When Jesus went out, He was going onto a spiritual battlefield in the fight of His life. When Jesus went out, He was relentlessly driving Himself for the sake of your soul.

When He went out, here's how He went.

"Jesus went out as usual. . ."

The phrase "as usual" means "as was His habit." Remember Jesus is going out to pray.

Jesus had made prayer habitual. Why is this so important that Luke had to include it in his account?

Spiritual habits get us supernatural help and hope!

This is why your commitment to be a desperado for Jesus is so huge. If you make it your habit to worship on the weekend, God makes it His habit to set up His throne in your week. If you want God constantly working everything together for the good in your life, then you consistently join His people in reckless worship.

The same is true of all your spiritual habits. If you consistently invest in relationships with other desperados, the Lord makes consistent investment in His relationship with you. If you are consistently in His Word, He consistently speaks into your life. If you make it your habit to serve others, God makes it His habit to serve you. If you are recklessly generous with the Lord out of your finances, the Lord is relentlessly generous to you with all that money cannot buy.

We will continue our Jesus story tomorrow. For now, let me share something special that happened while I was writing this book. My family was hanging out with a family from our church, when the young mom told us an exciting story. She was unemployed and looking for a part-time position in her field, so she could spend more time with her kids. But the only jobs available were full-time. This was made a matter of prayer.

When she came to church the next weekend, she had a $50 bill in her back pocket. Things had been tough financially with her out of work. That $50 was supposed to be for groceries for the upcoming week. During worship, she decided she wanted to be a desperado, recklessly pursuing a relentless Jesus. If she was going to be a desperado for Jesus, she was going to be all in. That's when she sensed God telling her to put the $50 in the offering. If she obeyed Him, He would more than take care of all her family's needs. She gave the $50. The next day she was offered a part-time position in her field. It was going to be a perfect fit for her family and their finances.

She lived the prayer, "Father, I place my life in Your hands" and learned the truth:

Spiritual habits get us supernatural help and hope!

THE DESPERADO DAILY

Ponder:

"While He lived on earth, anticipating death, Jesus cried out in pain and wept in sorrow as He offered up priestly prayers to God. Because He honored God, God answered Him. Though He was God's Son, He learned trusting-obedience by what He suffered, just as we do." (Hebrews 5:7,8 MSG)

Practice:

Freely practice spiritual habits of prayer, worship, Bible study and generosity, so the Lord is free to practice His supernatural help and hope in your life.

Pray:

"Father...not my will, but Yours be done. In Jesus' name, Amen."

DESPERADO

DAY 9

Surrender Everything?

"*JESUS WENT OUT as usual to the Mount of Olives....*" (Luke 22:39 NIV)

Evidently, Jesus had a friend who owned a garden on the Mount of Olives. "Hey, Jesus, anytime you need to get away. If you need a quiet place to pray, that garden is Yours." Jesus made it His habit to go there for prayer.

The garden was called "Gethsemane," which means "olive press." It was a grove of olive trees with an olive press, used to crush the olives for their oil. Isn't it intriguing that the Bible says, *"It was God's will to crush Him!"* (Isaiah 53:10)

This would be a completely thorough crushing. Crushed emotionally — it's like His heart is being ripped into pieces. Crushed relationally — even with His small group of friends present, Jesus had never been so utterly alone, painfully aware He'd soon be betrayed and abandoned. Crushed mentally — His mind was on fire with hellish thoughts of His coming crucifixion. All this contributed to a devastating physical crushing. Even His body betrayed Him, weakened beyond control. But the cruelest crushing happened on the deepest spiritual level — bearing our sin, becoming our sin, severed from His Father.

Jesus knew the crushing was coming, but for your sake and mine He walked right into this death-grip of agony. *"Jesus went out as usual to the Mount of Olives, and His disciples FOLLOWED Him."* (Luke 22:39 NIV)

This is huge for us, because everything in our lives is to be all about following Jesus. Why did Jesus have His personal desperados follow Him to this garden? What did He want them to see and hear? What did He want them to learn and experience? Why would He want them to witness the humiliating crushing? They'll have a ringside seat.

"He withdrew about a stone's throw beyond them." *(Luke 22:41 NIV)*

This would be very close by — maybe only 20 feet away, so they could watch and listen.

Here's what they saw and heard. *"Jesus plunged into agonizing sorrow. He said, 'This sorrow is crushing My life out!'"* (Matthew 26:38 MSG)

Do you ever feel like you're having the life crushed out of you? Has the life ever been crushed out of a dear relationship? Have you ever been crushed financially? Have you been through a mental, emotional, physical, spiritual crushing? What did you do? Here's what Jesus did. This was His habit when life got too hard and hurtful. *"Going a little farther, He fell with His face to the ground and prayed."* (Matthew 26:39)

He has them close, so they can hear His heart in prayer. He has us close, so we can understand all that His prayer means for us. It's Jesus' battle to stay relentless with His love. *"Father, if You are willing remove this cup from Me."* (Luke 22:42 ESV)

The term "cup" is a symbol for all of God's anger, all of God's judgment, all of God's condemnation. When Jesus goes to the cross, it's not just that He will be brutally executed. He would be, in fact, taking our place, as our substitute, to absorb on to Himself all the consequences of our sin — all God's wrath, all God's judgment, all God's condemnation due us for our sin. Jesus would literally be made our sin on the cross.

He's praying, "Father, is there any other way to save humanity than this all-consuming sacrifice? I cannot stand the thought of being made sin — of being consumed by Your anger, Your judgment, Your condemnation — of being separated from Your love. Is this the only way? Could there be some other option?"

Then comes the turning point. This is the prayer that releases all the power of God.

"Nevertheless, not My will, but Yours be done!" *(Luke 22:42 ESV)*

This is a prayer of full surrender. This is the secret of getting all of God's best for our lives — the best of His power, the best of His joy, the best of His peace, the best of His love.

When we surrender our everything, God gives us His everything!

This is the truth that turned the tide for Jesus. This was not a battle of whether to believe or not believe. This was a war of the wills. Would Jesus do as He wanted or would He surrender to what His Father wanted? Even under the horrific crushing, Jesus chooses God's will over His own. Because Jesus completely surrenders, He is given complete victory.

Jesus would later breathe these words over the heart of the Apostle Paul. *"Don't copy the behavior and customs of this world (which only and always wants what it wants, not giving a rip about what God wants) but let God transform you into a new person by changing the way you think. Then you will learn to know God's will for you, which is good and pleasing and perfect!"* (Romans 12:2 NLT)

In the garden, Jesus passionately and prayerfully surrendered His everything. So He got God's everything — resurrection power to conquer death, the grave and hell itself. He was exalted to the highest place and given the Name above all names. And by His prayer of full surrender, Jesus won His heart's ultimate desire — our salvation.

> *"During the days of Jesus' life on earth, He offered up prayers and petitions with loud cries and tears to the One who could save Him from death, and He was heard because of His reverent submission. Although He was a Son, He learned obedience from what He suffered and, once made perfect, He became the source of eternal salvation for all who obey Him."* (Hebrews 5:7-9 NIV)

What was true for Jesus is true for us. Surrender everything to get God's everything!

THE DESPERADO DAILY

Ponder:

> "Don't copy the behavior and customs of this world, but let God transform you into a new person by changing the way you think. Then you will learn to know God's will for you, which is good and pleasing and perfect." (Romans 12:2 NLT)

Practice:

> Prayerfully surrender everything you are and everything you have to receive God's everything for your life.

Pray:

> "Dear Father, You are Maker of heaven and earth. You are Sovereign God, large and in charge. You love me relentlessly and desire nothing but good for me. Yet surrender is so hard. It's like I want to be god of my life. I'm only good at making a mess of things. What You want for me is good, pleasing and perfect. Lord, please help me surrender everything to You. Help me trust you more. In Jesus' name, Amen."

DESPERADO
DAY 10

Invitation
to Be an
Image Bearer

SOMETIMES YOU CANNOT go forward without first going backward. That's our situation today. Before going forward to learn from one of the hardest seasons of Jesus' life, we must refocus on what had to be one of the happiest seasons of His life on earth.

I've always wondered if it all started on His thirtieth birthday. The age 30 carried important implications in the day of Jesus. At age 30, a priest was considered mature enough to begin to serve the Lord. At age 30, a rabbi was considered intelligent enough to teach God's Word. Was it on the morning of His thirtieth birthday that Jesus woke up to a keen sense of God's calling? I've always wondered.

Here's what we know for sure. *"Jesus Himself was about 30 years old, when He began His ministry!"* (Luke 3:23 NIV)

Here's what we know for sure. Jesus spent some days walking a distance of 60 miles to get from His home in Nazareth to the place in the Jordan River, where John the Baptist was burying people in the water in a spiritual experience called "baptism."

"Jesus came from Nazareth in Galilee and was baptized by John in the Jordan." (Mark 1:9 NIV)

This is what we know for sure. The very first thing Jesus did before He did any ministry — before He taught one lesson or healed one person or performed one miracle — the very first thing Jesus did was surrender to the spiritual experience of baptism.

Here's what I'm saying today. *Desperados follow Jesus into baptism.* This was a hugely significant experience for Jesus because, by His baptism, He brought pleasure to the heart of God. Baptism is a big deal experience for desperados, who desperately long to delight their Father in Heaven.

Desperados don't make excuses nor claim exemptions. Desperados don't try to talk themselves out of baptism nor let anyone else prevent them. Jesus wouldn't even let His own cousin, John the Baptist, slow Him down.

"Jesus then appeared, arriving at the Jordan River from Galilee. He wanted John to baptize Him. John objected, 'I'm the one who needs to be baptized, not You.' But Jesus insisted, 'Do it. God's work, putting things right...is coming together right now in this baptism.' So John did it." (Matthew 3:13-15 MSG)

Pleasing God, His Father, was more important to Jesus than anything. He would not begin one element of His ministry until He'd fully aligned His heart with what pleased the heart of God.

For Jesus, baptism came first!

But there is something else hugely significant at work here. *Jesus knew how to tap into the supernatural power of God for His life.* The power for miracles, for healings, for feeding the hungry and helping the hurting would only come from the Holy Spirit, who literally fluttered over Jesus at His baptism. *"The Holy Spirit descended on Him in bodily form like a dove."* (Luke 3:22 NIV)

The Apostle Peter said that the same Holy Spirit is available to us, when we're baptized.

"Be baptized, every one of you, in the name of Jesus Christ, for the forgiveness of your sins. And you will receive the gift of the Holy Spirit." (Acts 2:38 NIV)

Jesus set the example for all desperados and invites us each to follow Him into baptism.

Here's an important question: Is there proof of biblical desperados recklessly pursuing Jesus in baptism?

We find the answer to that question in Acts 2, when God shows up in power to birth His church. The Lord fires up Peter, who fires off this question to a gathered throng of thousands: "Do you remember that Jesus guy, who was right here in this city several weeks ago, the One you killed on a cross?" "Yeah, we remember. What of it?" "That Jesus was God's Son and God raised Him from the dead." "No way." "Yes way."

Peter pounds away at the proofs that Jesus was the Son of God.

"Let everyone know this: God has made this Jesus, whom you crucified, both Lord and Savior.' When the people heard this, they were cut to the heart and said to Peter, 'What shall we do?' Peter said, 'Change your life and be baptized, every one of you, in the name of Jesus Christ for the forgiveness of your sins. And you will receive the gift of the Holy Spirit.'" (Acts 2:38, 39 NIV)

That was the very first public presentation of the good news of Jesus. Here was the reckless response: **"Those who accepted his message were baptized, and about 3,000 were added to their number that day."** (Acts 2:41 NIV)

Thousands of first-time desperados did more than get wet when they went under the water. Their baptism changed their character and commitments, their priorities and values. By recklessly pursuing Jesus in baptism, they became more like Jesus.

The Apostle Paul wrote that we come into the family of God by our faith in Jesus. Once we surrender to Jesus as Lord, the first action we take, based on our belief, is to share fully in His death, burial and resurrection through baptism. We get more than wet. We begin to bear the image of Christ.

"You are sons of God through faith in Christ Jesus, for all of you who were baptized into Christ have clothed yourselves with Christ!" (Galatians 3:26,27 NIV)

Desperados are reckless to do whatever it takes to make Jesus look good in their lives.

THE DESPERADO DAILY

Ponder:

"You are sons of God through faith in Christ Jesus, for all of you who were baptized into Christ have clothed yourselves with Christ!" (Galatians 3:26,27 NIV)

Practice:

Let your greatest desire be to bring pleasure to the heart of God. Be baptized, then spend every breath recklessly pursuing your relentless Jesus.

Pray:

"Dear Jesus, thank You for exemplifying how to bring pleasure to the heart of God.

I want to follow Your example in all things, Lord. Obviously, for You, Jesus, baptism came first. Then You did life in the power of the Holy Spirit. God has been nothing but good to me every day of my life. All I care about is doing life powered by the Holy Spirit and making glad the heart of our Heavenly Father. In Your name, Amen."

DESPERADO

DAY 11

The Holy Spirit Comes in Power

WHEN WAS THE last time you were absolutely devastated — so devastated that you were at the very end of yourself physically, emotionally, mentally and spiritually? Have you ever been so devastated that you just go numb or you don't even feel like eating? What mattered to you before the devastation does not seem important at all now. What is the most devastating experience you have ever had to live through?

You find the lump. You have the biopsy. You get the phone call. It's cancer. If that wasn't devastating enough, you endure mastectomy, chemo and radiation. You lose your hair. It's like one devastation piled on another.

Or maybe your spouse does not love you anymore — doesn't want to be with you anymore. They've found someone else — someone more interesting, younger, thinner, more exciting, someone easier to love. In the face of all that, they want the house, and, most devastating of all, they want the kids. It's like one devastation piled on another.

Or maybe it was that long season of devastation, when you had lost a child. You didn't know if you would ever recover. Or maybe your spouse of many, many years is dying; or maybe you have a parent with Alzheimer's — perfectly healthy, just mentally gone. Or maybe you have a child with a mental illness. These are not devastations that you sprint through; these are like devastation decathlons. It's like one devastating event after another and you're not any good at any of them.

Or maybe you weren't devastated by something that happened. You were devastated by someone who hurt you — lied to you, cheated on you, betrayed you, rejected you, abused you, talked about you behind your back, said horrible things to your face. It was emotionally devastating. It's mentally devastating, because you can't stop thinking about it. Every time you replay it in your head, you repeat the devastation in your heart.

To me, the worst kind of devastation I've suffered has not been caused by something or someone. The devastation I hate the most is what I bring on myself. I told the lie and got caught. Now I'm not trusted. I made the promise and did not keep it. Now I have no credibility. I said the hurtful words and wrecked the relationship. I did the wrong thing at the wrong time. I made my bed. Now I have to lay in it. I created my own painful devastation. The devastation I hate the most is the one I make for myself.

Did you know there's an actual place on our planet called "the devastation?" It looks just the way we feel when we're going through devastation — barren, desolate, lifeless, a waste land. Hold on to that mental image a second. Is that what your marriage looks like? Is that what your singleness feels like? Is that your financial status? Is that a good image for your heart when you are living in the devastation?

I have a story for you today. This story is the best good news you'd ever want to hear when you suffer a bad devastation. This is a Jesus story. This is a story of Jesus striding strategically into the very place called the "devastation". Jesus marched, head held high, into His own personal devastation — on purpose — for three big reasons.

First, this is irrefutable evidence that Jesus is willing to join you in your devastation. He isn't afraid of your devastation. He is not put off by your devastation. He's not repulsed by your devastation. Jesus loves you so much He is drawn to your devastation.

Secondly, Jesus entered the worst possible kind of devastation to show us how to get through whatever devastates us. Jesus exemplifies not just how to cope, but how to conquer any and every devastating situation. Our tendency is to be overwhelmed. Jesus shows us how to actually overcome the devastation.

Third and most important, Jesus intentionally entered His deadly devastation to utterly defeat the evil that too often defeats us. He victoriously cut a perfect path through the devastation to show us the way to win anytime evil tries to devastate us.

Let me set the scene of this Jesus story. Jesus has just been baptized in the Jordan River. A series of significant events unfold at the baptism of Jesus. First, Jesus is praying. I wonder what He was talking to God about. Maybe He was praying, "My Father in heaven, I humble myself before you in baptism. I want all who follow Me to see the significance of this spiritual experience. I want to do what's right in your eyes. I want to know that I'm doing exactly what You want me to do."

I wonder if Jesus was praying somewhat along these lines, because look what happens. *"As He was praying, heaven was opened and the Holy Spirit descended on Him in bodily form like a dove. And a Voice came from heaven; 'You are My Son, whom I love; with You I am well pleased.'"* (Luke 3:21-22 NIV)

Notice all three members of the Godhead are engaged. Jesus prays. The Holy Spirit comes in power. God the Father speaks, confirming that when Jesus is baptized, He is doing what's right in God's eyes. The baptism of Jesus is a call for us to follow Him in this spiritual experience, sharing in His death, burial and resurrection.

Now we're ready for what happens next in our Jesus story. *"Jesus, full of the Holy Spirit..."* (Luke 4:1 NIV)

Jesus was going to absolutely dominate in His personal devastation, because He was full of the Holy Spirit. Jesus would come under intense attack at the worst possible time in the worst possible place. He would be overwhelmingly victorious, because He was full of the Holy Spirit.

The same is true of us. The only way we can power our way through any devastation is to be full of the Holy Spirit. The only way to be full of the Holy Spirit is to recklessly follow our relentless Jesus, who gives us an unshakable promise and a life-giving purpose: *"You will receive power, when the Holy Spirit comes upon you. And you will be My witnesses, telling people about Me everywhere!"* (Acts 1:8 NLT)

THE DESPERADO DAILY

Ponder:

> "You will receive power, when the Holy Spirit comes upon you. And you will be My witnesses, telling people about Me everywhere!" (Acts 1:8 NLT)

Practice:

Follow Jesus into any devastation. Be filled with the Holy Spirit. Find God's favor by faithfully doing whatever He calls you to do.

Pray:

"Dear Jesus, thank You for joining me in my devastation. Please fill me with the Holy Spirit. I need a strength and wisdom greater than myself. Lord, I believe You are making a way for me to get through what I'm going through. In Your name, Amen."

DESPERADO

DAY 12

Fully Loved
Just as You Are

THERE IS A universe of difference between how we are filled with the Holy Spirit and how Jesus was filled with the Holy Spirit.

Jesus was literally born full of the Holy Spirit. Here's how the angel Gabriel promised it to Mary the mother of Jesus. "The Holy Spirit will get you pregnant by the supernatural power of the Heavenly Father, so the baby born to you will be the Son of God."

Not only was Jesus born full of the Holy Spirit, there was not a moment of His life on earth when He was not full of the Holy Spirit. Jesus was always full of the Holy Spirit.

Jesus was born of woman, so He was fully human. Jesus was born by the Holy Spirit, so He was at the very same time fully God. This made Him the only qualified candidate to die as full payment for our sins and be raised from the dead to the glory of the Father.

Scripture tells us that when we are baptized, our sins are forgiven and we are filled with the Holy Spirit (Acts 2:38). The big trouble with us is that we leak. That's why Paul tells the believers in Ephesus, "Keep being filled by the Holy Spirit." We don't stay filled with the Holy Spirit 24/7. We must pray for the Holy Spirit to fill us.

Every day I want to pray for myself and the church I serve, *"I keep asking that the God of our Lord Jesus Christ, the glorious Father, may give you the Spirit of wisdom and revelation, so that you may know Him better."* (Ephesians. 1:17 NIV)

With this in mind let's get back to our story. *"Jesus, full of the Holy Spirit, returned from the Jordan and was led by the Spirit in the desert."* (Luke 4:1 NIV)

The Hebrew word for this desert is "jeshimon". It means "the devastation". This is an ugly wasteland — 35 miles long, 15 miles wide, filled with steep cliffs and narrow ravines. This brutal, barren wilderness is a place for snakes, scorpions and little else.

Why would the Holy Spirit lead Jesus into this deadly devastation? First, you cannot see the Holy Spirit as forcing Jesus to go. Jesus and the Holy Spirit are both excited to be going into the devastation. They have anticipated this moment together forever.

The baptism of Jesus was His first step towards His death on the cross. Entering the desert was His second step. He was going there on purpose with full intention of utterly and totally defeating the devil. This would be a critical, spiritual devastation, *"Where for 40 days He was tempted by the devil."* (Luke 4:2)

Guess what the Greek word for the devil is? "Diabolos!" In Spanish it's "diablo". To tell the truth, this is exciting to me. In this account, we learn how **desperados can defeat diablo in any devastation!**

So far in our study we've seen how the relentless love of Jesus comes to us, how the relentless prayers of Jesus go up for us. Now we see how the relentless power of Jesus goes before us to provide the very best victory in even the worst devastation.

Here's how devastating the devastation was to Jesus. *"Jesus ate nothing during those days, and at the end of them He was hungry."* (Luke 4:2 NIV)

24/7, for nearly six weeks, Jesus doesn't even have food on His radar. He is relentless in showing His absolute dominance over Diablo. Jesus keeps pounding away, pounding away, pounding away at Diablo until finally there's a big breakthrough. That is when He starts to think about food again.

Over these forty days we are not exactly sure how Diablo was attacking Jesus or how Jesus counter-attacked. What we know for sure is how Diablo makes this last ditch desperate effort to devastate Jesus. This is hugely important for us because this is how Diablo attacks us when we enter a devastation.

Diablo dishes out doubt!

This is how he does it to Jesus. Diablo senses the vulnerability of Jesus. He grabs a rock and gets up in the face of Jesus and sneers, *"If you are the Son of God, tell this stone to become bread."* (Luke 4:5 NIV)

Notice that when we are in a devastation, the first thing Diablo wants to do is get us to doubt our core identity as children of God. He puts one doubting "if" after another in our heads. "If you were a better Christian...if you were a better mother...if you were a better husband...

if you were a better friend...if God really does care about you..."

Notice how Diablo calls into question the core identity of Jesus. *"If you are the Son of God."* Jesus certainly is the Son of God. Over 150 times in The New Testament Jesus is called the Son of God.

But here is what is so significant in this war of words between Diablo and our relentless Jesus. Remember how God the Father addressed His Son. I love the way the ESV handles it, when God says to Jesus, *"You are my beloved Son, with you I am well pleased."* (Luke 3:22 ESV)

Notice what Diablo conveniently leaves out — that Jesus is the "beloved" Son of God. He is dishing out doubt after doubt after doubt about the love relationship between God the Father and Jesus, His one and only Son. Diablo tries to do the same thing to every desperado. He dishes out doubts that you are fully loved by God just as you are.

Here's the absolute truth about desperados for Jesus: *"Those who are led by the Spirit of God are sons of God. For you did not receive a spirit that makes you a slave again to fear, but you received the Spirit of sonship....The Spirit Himself testifies with our spirit that we are God's children."* (Romans 8:14-16 NIV)

THE DESPERADO DAILY

Ponder:

> "*Those who are led by the Spirit of God are sons of God. For you did not receive a spirit that makes you a slave again to fear, but you received the Spirit of sonship.... The Spirit Himself testifies with our spirit that we are God's children.*" (Romans 8:14-16 NIV)

Practice:

> Anchor your soul to the truth of your core identity in Christ as a beloved, pleasing child of the Father. You will destroy the doubts dished out by Diablo..

Pray:

> "*Dear Jesus, You are the beloved Son of the living God. Following You leads me into a real relationship with the Father, by Whom I am deeply loved and fully favored. Doubts will arise, but You will help me destroy Diablo's lies with the truth of who You are and who I am as a constantly cared-for child of the Father. In Your name, Amen.*"

DESPERADO
DAY 13

Humility Reigns

DOUBTS ARE THE disease of the soul. They create dis-ease in our relationship with God. Mild doubts are like a cold or the flu. Everyone suffers from them. But if a doubt gets malignant and goes untreated, it can be a spiritual cancer, eating away at our reckless pursuit of Jesus.

I should know. I should be an expert on doubt. From my personal experience, I can tell when dark doubts start to infect my faith. The first symptom I show is asking the wrong question. Why? Why me? Why did this happen? Why, why, why is wah, wah, wah.

But now I know the cure. Now I know the right questions that dispel all my doubts in no time. Several years ago, I had a painful case of discouraging doubt. I was so frustrated by the pressure of ministry, the strain of being the leader and the stress of feeling stuck. I felt like I was doing my part. Why wasn't God doing His?

But our Lord is so good, even when we are clueless. In His faithfulness, the Father put me in the front row of a conference where the speaker asked two questions. I can't tell you anything else he said. But I'll never forget the two questions. Is God good? Can God be trusted? Yes! Yes! Yes! Yes! Boom! Doubts defeated. Doubts gone!

It was a defining moment in my faith. Doubts still creep onto the back burner of my brain. But now, every time I sense the first symptoms of doubt-disease, I shout; I sigh; I sing: "God is good! God can be trusted. That's the truth that sets me free of doubt!"

When the evil one dishes out doubts, every doubt is a lie. But guess what. Desperados defeat the lies of Diablo with the truth of God, all based on the premise that God is good and God can be trusted. Diablo doesn't have a chance against us as long as we stay anchored to God's truth.

That's what Jesus did in His devastation, when Satan challenged His unique identity. *"'If You are the Son of God, tell this stone to become bread.' Jesus answered, "Man does not live by bread alone, but on every word that comes from the mouth of God."* (Luke 4:4, Mt. 4:4)

Jesus is quoting Deuteronomy 8:3. He defeats the lies of Diablo with God's truth. Here is how I've heard it said that helps me: "Doubt your doubts and believe your beliefs."

But Diablo is not done trying to devastate Jesus. *"The devil led Him up to a high place and showed Him in an instant all the kingdoms in the world. And he said to Him, "I will give you all their authority and splendor, for it has been given to me, and I can give it to anyone I want to. So if you worship me, it will be yours."* (Luke 4:5-7)

Diablo specializes in deceit!

Diablo says he's in charge of the world and he will give the world to Jesus, if only Jesus will bow before him in worship. This Diablo claims as his own what does not in any way belong to him. Only God is in charge of the world. And God has given all authority in Heaven and earth to Jesus. That's the truth.

Diablo will always try to lay claim to what is not his own — our families and friends, our finances, our feelings, even our faith. His intention is to destroy by deceit. Jesus said of Diablo, *"The thief only comes to steal and kill and destroy."* (John 10:10 NIV)

Diablo is no match for Jesus. This isn't even a fight. Jesus knows that everything we gain physically, financially, relationally or emotionally we win through worship. We worship our way out of any devastation. We worship our way into abundance of faith, hope, love, strength, wisdom, peace and joy. That's the promise of Jesus. (John 10:10)

Once again, Jesus defeats Diablo with the truth of God's Word. *"Jesus answered, "It is written: "Worship the Lord your God and serve Him only."* (Luke 4:8 NIV)

Even when you find yourself in a devastation, keep worshipping, keep serving God. Worship keeps you stronger than any devastation life throws your way. Devastations are unavoidable. But serving others is the shortest and surest way to victory.

Diablo in his persistence takes one more shot at Jesus. *"The devil led Him to Jerusalem and had Him stand on the highest point of the temple. "If you are the Son of God," he said, "throw yourself down from here. For it is written:' He will command His angels concerning you to guard you carefully; they will lift you up in their hands, so that you will not strike your foot against a stone."* Luke 4:9-11

Diablo specializes in distrust!

Diablo throws Holy Scripture in Jesus' face. Jesus had used God's Word to defeat Diablo. Now Diablo uses what God has promised to lure Jesus into the trap of not trusting the utter goodness of God.

Satan is hissing at Jesus, "If You are God's Son, tell Your Father to put up or shut up. Call Your Father's bluff. He has promised You protection. Make Him prove it."

Jesus is straight-forward, wasting little effort as He gives Old Diablo a serious spiritual beatdown, *"Jesus answered, 'It says: Do not put the Lord your God to the test.'"* (Luke 4:12 NIV)

Jesus pounded Diablo with serious, repeated body blows of God's Word. The evil one cannot stand up against such truth. He slithers away to lick his wounds. *When the devil had finished all this tempting, he left until an opportune time."* (Luke 4:12-13)

Jesus and Satan are more than opposites. They are diametrically opposed to each other in every way. Jesus is the Truth. Satan is a liar. But the most glaring difference between our Lord and the vile evil one is how they speak to and about God.

Check out Diablo's bluster, *"'I WILL ascend to heaven...I WILL raise my throne...I WILL ascend above...I WILL make myself like the Most High!'"* (Isaiah 14:12-14)

On the other hand, Jesus humbly prays, *"Not My will, but Yours be done."* (Luke 22:42)

Satan makes his proclamation in heaven and is cast down to hell. Jesus relentlessly cries out in a garden and is exalted to the right hand of God. Desperados recklessly pursue the example of their relentless Jesus.

THE DESPERADO DAILY

Ponder:

> "The thief (diablo) comes only to steal and kill and de-
> stroy. I (Jesus) came that they may have life and have it
> abundantly." (John 10:10 ESV)

Practice:

Defeat every doubt with the truth: God is good and
God can be trusted!

Pray:

> "Dear Lord, thank You for going into a wilderness war
> with Diablo in my behalf. You defeated the evil deceiver
> with the truth of God's Word. May God's Word always
> be my strength. Your Word is my hope and strength. In
> Your name, Amen."

DESPERADO
DAY 14

Being Made
Better Than Good

I DON'T REMEMBER how the fight started, but I knew I was about to take the beating of my young life. It was right before ninth grade basketball practice. It had not been much of a fight. The boy on top of me was bigger, stronger, quicker and meaner than me. He found me someone easy to bully during most of the time we knew each other. Presently, he had me flat on my back, his knees on my shoulders, one hand on my throat and one fist drawn back to pound my face.

Remarkably, he did something totally unexpected. He did not hit me even once. I wish he had. He leaned down nose-to-nose with me, sneered and said, "You're not worth the trouble. You're only a third-string guard. You're not good enough to mess with." His words did more damage than his fists ever could.

I scraped myself off the gym floor with a new painful truth scratched across my soul, "You're not good enough."

Have you ever been there? Do you have a life-time membership in the "you're not good enough" club? Maybe you weren't a kid like me — an easy target for bullies. Maybe you were the bully. Maybe you took your beatings at home. Maybe your dad had a vicious temper. He took it out on you and your mom. Every time he hit you, you got the message, "You're not good enough." Then you spent much of your time looking for people to beat up. You might not be good enough, but at least you're better than someone you could knock around.

We all go through life chased by that "you're not good enough" demon. You're not smart enough, rich enough, popular enough, athletic enough. You're not good looking enough, tall enough, skinny enough. You're not good enough.

You go through your whole life trying as hard as you can — at church, at work, at marriage, at raising kids, at making money, at making friends — but most of the time coming up empty. You can't shake the feeling. You're not good enough.

About fifteen years ago I had that ugly truth drilled into me one more painful time. My wife and I had given everything we had to adopting a child from Haiti. He was a boy we had fallen in love with. His name was Wilky. We didn't think twice about investing all our money, all our emotion, all our prayers in an all-out effort to make Wilky our son.

We were very hopeful, when we were invited into the U.S. immigration office in Port au Prince, Haiti. We were prayed up. We'd filled out our forms and paid our money, including too many bribes to count. We were American citizens. We were Christians. It was all going to work out. We felt like we'd been slugged in the stomach when we were informed that Wilky, under no circumstances, would ever be allowed to leave Haiti and come to the U.S. as our son.

An I.N.S. agent was explaining legal technicalities to me, when I interrupted him, "This child is our son. His adoption has the approval of the Haitian government." The agent said, "This is never going to happen. Just get back on a plane, go back to America and forget you ever met this boy." I said, "We are now legally his parents in Haiti. We're responsible for his education and well-being." The agent across the table from me said, "No one is going to hold you to that or come looking for you. People abandon children in Haiti all the time."

With that we were ushered back out onto the street. The car ride back to the orphanage was the longest of my life. Our Haitian attorney was in tears. At the orphanage, the 12x12 cinderblock room where we stayed had a mattress on the floor. Deb and I threw ourselves on it and wept. We felt like we were drowning in an oppressive darkness that laughed at us, "You're not good enough."

I've often wondered if Peter felt like he was drowning in that same oppressive darkness. There was only one thing Peter was good at — catching fish. The life of a commercial fisherman was not a bad life. You got to work outdoors. You had great friends. You could make a decent living, if you were good enough. But the day I'm talking about was the morning Peter was choking on the fear that he wasn't even good enough at the only thing he knew to do.

All the evidence he needed was the empty boat in which he sat — the empty nets dangling in his hands. He, his brother and his partners had fished all night. They did their best. They did everything they knew to do.

Still they came up empty. Evidently, they just weren't good enough.

How was Peter going to put food on the table with an empty boat and empty nets? He was still paying for the boat. His mother-in-law had just moved in with them. How was he going to explain this to his wife? How could he tell her he simply wasn't good enough? He was doomed to live a little life.

Let's fast-forward beyond the crucifixion and resurrection of Jesus, when, as a desperado, Peter writes for all desperados.

> *"All praise to God, the Father of our Lord Jesus Christ. It is by His great mercy that we have been born again, because God raised Jesus Christ from the dead. Now we live with great expectation, and we have a priceless inheritance that is kept in heaven for you, pure and undefiled, beyond the reach of change or decay. And through your faith God is protecting you by His power until you receive this salvation, which is ready to be revealed on the last day for all to see. So be truly glad. There is wonderful joy ahead, even though you must endure many trials for a little while. These trials will show that your faith is genuine.... When your faith remains strong through the many trials, it will bring you much praise and glory and honor at the appearing of Jesus Christ!" (I Peter 1:3-7 NLT)*

In our story Peter is about to learn the secret of being made better than good.

THE DESPERADO DAILY

Ponder:

"When your faith remains strong through the many trials. It will bring you much praise and glory and honor at the appearing of Jesus Christ." (I Peter 1:7 NLT)

Practice:

Cancel your membership in the "not good enough" club. Claim your reality as a desperado for Jesus: "There is wonderful joy ahead, even though you must endure many trials for a little while."

Pray:

"Dear Lord Jesus, thank You for joining me in this life of hurt and hardship. Thank You for working everything together for good in my life, not based on anything good in me, but on the fact that You are infinite goodness. Thank You for making me good enough by Your good work on the cross. You give me Your goodness. In Your name, Amen!"

DESPERADO
DAY 15

Not,
Not Good Enough

FROM PETER'S PRESENT perspective, coming back to shore in an empty boat — empty-handed, empty-hearted, living an empty life — he was never going to be somebody big.

In his time, the first century A.D., the most important somebodies were rabbis. If you had any hope of ever being somebody big, you had to be a rabbi's disciple. That had not panned out for Peter.

Every little Jewish boy got his shot at the big time. They went to what we might call grade school, where they were to learn the first five books of the Bible. When they got through the grades, only the best got to go on to what we might call high school, where they were to memorize the entire Old Testament. When it was time to graduate, the best of the best would interview with a rabbi. Only those good enough would be called to be the rabbi's disciples. Only those good enough had a shot at being somebody big.

If you couldn't cut it, the Rabbi might say, "You'd be better off going back home and learning the family trade, like fishing." If the rabbi thought you were good enough, he'd say, "I think you have it in you to be like me. I think you have it in you to do what I do. Come. Follow me." That's how a rabbi called his disciples.

That had never happened to Peter. He had never made the cut. He wasn't good enough, so he fished. His life had shrunk down to the size of an empty boat. He just wasn't good enough — never had been, never would be.

Have you ever had thoughts like that? I'm just not good enough — never have been, never will be. Only the worst ever happens to me. I never get a break.

Maybe what happened to Peter needs to happen to you. Do you know what happened to Peter? Jesus knocked on the side of his boat.

Peter looked up from his nets and there was Jesus, standing in knee-deep water beside his boat. "Hey, Peter, do you mind if I use your boat as a pulpit? Look at the size of this crowd, aching to hear the Word of God."

Peter saw the crowd and hoped no one noticed his boat empty of fish. Other boats were pulled ashore. Other fishermen had caught fish. Other fishermen had food for their family. Other fishermen had the dignity of being good enough.

Peter said, "Yes, Lord. You may use my boat. It's not good for much else." Jesus climbed aboard. I wonder if the atmosphere changed inside the boat when Jesus got on board. I wonder if Peter noticed anything but his empty nets.

Coincidentally, at the very same time Peter had the nets cleaned and stowed away, Jesus finished teaching. Jesus turned to Peter and said, "Hey, I've got a great idea.

Let's go fishing." Peter just looked at Him like He was crazy. Jesus said, *"Put out into deep water, and let down the nets for a catch."* (Luke 5:4 NIV)

"Now, with all these people watching, could You ask me to do anything more embarrassing? Any fisherman knows you don't fish in deep water. This is the wrong time of day to catch anything. I can't believe this. You're asking me to cast not just one net, but nets. This is crazy." I think those might have been the thoughts banging around in Peter's brain. But here's what came out of his mouth, *"Master, we've worked hard all night and haven't caught anything. But because you say so, I will let down the nets."* (Luke 5:5 NIV)

This becomes a defining moment in Peter's life. He doesn't want to go fishing. He doesn't feel like fishing. At that moment he hates the very thought of fishing. But Peter is willing to obey Jesus no matter how he feels.

Here's what Peter did. He pushed out into deep water. Back out of the tackle box came the newly cleaned nets — not net, but nets, and at this crazy time of day.

Well-practiced hands unfurled the nets and flung them over the sea, where they hovered for just a moment, like webbed Frisbees defying gravity. Then smack, they slapped the surface of the water, and some unseen force yanked them fiercely out of sight. The ropes attached to the nets started zipping into the sea. Without thinking, calloused hands seized the ropes. Knobby, fishermen knees banged the side of the boat. Muscled arms disappeared into the water. Pull. The boat tips up on its side. Fishermen strain for all they're worth. The nets won't budge. "Help." They call out to their partners. "Fish."

Another boat slides up alongside them. More hands dive into the water. Pull. The nets now literally begin to tear. Hands dig down into the nets and haul out fish. Boats pile up with fish.

Suddenly, Peter stops, lets go of the net and looks at Jesus, who's standing in the bow of the boat, smiling, "Told you." Peter wades knee-deep through fish until he gets to Jesus, where he kneels and says, "Lord, get out of my boat. Get out of my life. I'm a sin-filled loser." Now, Peter isn't telling Jesus to jump in the lake. When he welcomed Jesus into his boat, he called him Master. Now when he bows before Him in worship, Peter calls Jesus "Lord". "You are God. I am not. You are good. I am not."

I absolutely love the next thing that happens. Jesus will not leave Peter down on his face. He won't leave Peter's soul scarred with the words, "Not good enough." Jesus lifts Peter to his feet, looks him in the eye and says, "Don't be afraid. You have it in you to be like Me. You have it in you to do what I do. Come follow Me."

THE DESPERADO DAILY

Ponder:

"Shake off your complacency and repent. See, I stand knocking at the door. If anyone listens to My voice and opens the door, I will go into his house, and dine with him, and he with Me. As for the victorious, I will give him the honor of sitting beside Me on My throne, just as I Myself have won the victory..." (Revelation 3:19-21 Phillips NT)

Practice:

Answer His call when Jesus knocks on the side of your boat. Let Him make you victorious in all you do.

Pray:

"Jesus, my Master, I humble myself before You. You are God and I am not. You are good and I am not. I praise You that our relationship is not based on how good I am. Thank You for believing in me. You believe I have it in me to be like You and do what You do. Lord, I will follow You with all my heart. In Your precious, saving name, Amen."

DESPERADO
DAY 16

The Kiss of Grace

CAN YOU GET a feel for what Peter felt? What do you think it did to him when Jesus said, "I think you've got it in you to do what I do. I think you've got it in you to be like Me"? What would you give to have Jesus say that to you? That's exactly what He wants to sigh over your soul right now, as He calls you to follow Him.

I wonder at some point in the process of calling Peter, if Jesus didn't lean in and give him a kiss on the neck. I don't know that that happened.

Later in His ministry Jesus tells a story about a young man who runs off with what amounts to one-third of all his dad's money. He takes the money and moves as far away from his dad as he can. Then in that far off place this rebellious son blows through his dad's hard-earned money like it's nothing. He wastes it all.

When he runs out of money, he runs out of self-respect and says, "I've sinned against God. I've sinned against my father. I'm no longer good enough to be my father's son. But maybe if I go home, my father will give me a job." He heads for home. All the way home he rehearses the speech, "Dad, I've sinned against God. I've sinned against you. I'm no longer good enough to be your son. But would you be willing just to give me a job?" It was the longest walk of his life.

But, guess who's waiting back home, waiting and watching. There's an anxious Father, hoping for his son to return. In fact, as soon as he sees his son crest a distant hill, the father takes off on a dead-run. Here's how Jesus tells it: *"When he was yet a great way off, his father saw him, and had compassion, and ran, and fell on his neck, and kissed him."* (Luke 15:20 KJV)

You be that son just for a moment. You turn to God and He comes running to meet you. You feel like you're not good enough, but God has a kiss for you. Personally, I have experienced that kiss myself. I know what it feels like.

Let me explain by confessing my regret over my failures as a father. It has to do with how I tried to raise my older, biological boys. I tried to raise them the way I was raised. It blew up in my face. They did not respond well to it. They rebelled against it, and rightly so. They were not me. And I was not my mom and dad.

There were times after I'd had an angry incident with my sons, I'd go out in the backyard and cry. Why was I such a jerk? I felt like I was way too impatient, too angry, too punitive, not enough understanding, not enough compassion, not enough grace. I carried a lot of shame over how I treated my sons.

My sons would never say that. My sons would call me a great dad. We have a great relationship. They're my best friends. I have apologized to them for being such a jerk and they've said, "Get over it, Dad." But I couldn't get over it.

Until one Sunday afternoon our family was together for dinner. After we had eaten, I was on the couch, probably watching a ballgame. As Josh was gathering up his family to go home, he came and leaned over me. I thought he'd give me a hug, but he kissed me on the neck.

I'm sure for Josh it was just a kiss. But for me it was so much more. I'll never forget what that kiss felt like. With that kiss I felt forgiven. With that kiss my shame melted away. That kiss was amazing. That kiss was grace. That kiss healed me like nothing else could. Everybody needs that kind of kiss.

Like my adopted son, Wilky. Here's the rest of his story. A year after that bad meeting with the I.N.S., we were still doing everything possible to get our son into the U.S. Unfortunately, he was hit by a car and his left femur was broken. Unbelievably, that's exactly what God used to bring Wilky to our home.

Two weeks after coming to America Wilky had surgery to repair his broken femur.

The orthopedic surgeon did it for free and Rockford Memorial Hospital provided all medical services for free.

That happened in October. By spring of the next year, Wilky was fully recovered, with surgical scars up his thigh and down across his knee. But he was doing great — doing great physically, doing great in school. He was our gift from God.

Wilky asked me one day if he could buy some new shorts, so I said, "Let's go shopping." Since his favorite color is orange, we were looking for orange shorts.

Orange shorts are a rare commodity. We went from store to store with no luck. Finally, when we found a pair, Wilky tried them on. They came down to his knee. He said, "No thanks. Let's go home."

On the way home, feeling kind of weird about the whole thing, I say, "Wilky, you wanted some orange shorts." "Yes." "Well, we found some." "So." "Wilky, why didn't we buy those shorts?" "I didn't want them." "Wilky, it wasn't because they didn't cover up your scars, was it? Wilky, you're not embarrassed of your scars, are you?" I look over at him and a tear is rolling down his cheek.

I pull over to the side of the road. Now I'm bawling. I say, "Son, if it wasn't for your surgery, you would never have come to America. If it was not for your scars, you wouldn't be with Mom and Dad. Your scars put you in our home. I love your scars. I thank God for your scars. I'll kiss your scars." And I did.

When Jesus calls us, He calls us scars and all. He calls us to kiss our scars. In fact, it's our scars that make us irresistible to Jesus. When He calls us, Jesus drives away all the "not good enough" demons. Jesus calls to every desperado, "You've got it in you to be like Me. You've got in you to do what I do. Come, follow Me."

THE DESPERADO DAILY

···

Ponder:

> "But while he was a long way off, his Father saw him
> and was filled with compassion for him; He ran to His
> son, threw His arms around him and kissed him." (Luke
> 15:20 NIV)

Practice:

> To experience God's forgiveness and healing, humble
> yourself; pray; turn from your wicked ways and seek
> God's face.

Pray:

> "Dear Father, thank You for never taking Your eyes
> off me. Again, I praise You for never giving up on me.
> I return to You with all my heart. Where would I be
> without Your compassion? I long to be in Your arms,
> kissed by Your grace. In Jesus name, Amen."

DESPERADO
DAY 17

The Lord of Life

GROWTH IS EVERYTHING, because growth is an indication of true health!

A growing marriage is a healthy marriage. A growing friendship is a healthy friendship. You grow emotionally when you are emotionally healthy. You grow mentally when you are mentally healthy. When you have a healthy financial plan, you will have growing finances. We grow as parents as we do healthy parenting.

I could go on and on with example after example. But here's the bottom line. *Growth is an indication of true health. But true health is always a choice!*

Here's my deeply-held conviction — *True health happens in our lives when we make the choice to follow Jesus, the Lord of life!*

True health happens in a family when we choose to follow Jesus, the Lord of life, in our family. True health happens in our parenting when we choose to follow Jesus, the Lord of life, in our parenting. In our emotional struggles, when we choose to follow Jesus, the Lord of life, He leads us into peace, joy, and hope. True health happens in our finances when we choose to follow Jesus, the Lord of life, in our finances.

I'm about to assert something very disturbing. Most people do not choose to follow Jesus, the Lord of life. *Most people choose to follow the lord of death.*

Most people follow the lord of death in their marriage and the marriage dies. Most people follow the lord of death in their emotions and their emotions go dead — no peace, no hope, no joy. They follow the lord of death in their thinking and their minds go very dark. In whatever area of life we choose to follow the lord of death, that area of our life goes dead. Even churches can go dead. Even church-goers can have a dead faith.

The church I serve has made the most life-giving choice possible. We say it this way: *Everything in my life, everything in our church is to be all about following Jesus —* nothing more, nothing less, nothing else. We absolutely refuse to follow the lord of death.

Let me explain all of this by telling you a Jesus story. But before I get to the story, I have to tell you about the story-teller. The truth is he's more than a teller of stories. He's a remarkably accurate historian. He records historical events. His name is Luke, but I call him one of the most dynamic desperados of all time.

In terms of sheer volume, his writing of Luke and Acts makes up more of the New Testament than any other author. He was so reckless in his pursuit of our relentless Jesus that we now have his account of the life, death, and resurrection of Jesus, as well as the miraculous movement of the Holy Spirit throughout the life of the church when it was exactly as God intended it to be.

Luke's life choice was to follow Jesus, the Lord of life. He made a living as a physician, but he made a life by following Jesus, the Lord of life. Luke wrote more about Jesus than anyone else. In fact, this whole set of daily desperado devotions is based on the stories, prayers, and teachings of Jesus that can only be found in Luke. He saw what others did not see. He heard what others did not hear. He felt what others did not feel. And he wrote it down under the breath of God, for us.

Let's see how humbly Luke introduces himself and his passionate purpose:

> "Many have undertaken to draw up an account of the things that have been fulfilled among us, just as they were handed down to us by those who from the first were eyewitnesses and servants of the Word. Therefore, since I myself have carefully investigated everything from the beginning, it seemed good also to me to write an orderly account for you, most excellent Theophilus, so that you may know the certainty of the things you have been taught." (Luke 1:1-4 NIV)

Luke never calls himself by name in this lengthy introduction. He does not try to impress us with his credentials as a physician; he wants us to be impressed with his careful investigation of everything about Jesus from the beginning. He personally interviewed eyewitnesses. He made every effort to organize it all in the right order.

I hope it doesn't hurt your feelings, but Luke was not thinking about you or me, or the billions of other Christ-followers on the planet, as he did this incredible work. Luke got the specific names right, the specific places right, the specific dates right, the specific events of the life of Jesus right, all for one man named Theophilus. What Luke wanted more than anything was for his friend, Theophilus, to keep choosing to follow Jesus, the Lord of life.

Who is your Theophilus? Who is the special person in your life whom you would love to see choose to have a real relationship with Jesus? You decided to follow the Lord of life. Talk about experiencing true health. All your sins are forgiven — past, present and even future sins. You've been cleansed of all guilt and shame. You have access to all the promises of God. You can be fully confident of God working for your good. What friends or family do you want to see find what you've found in following the Lord of life?

Luke wanted to do heaven with Theophilus. Luke could not stand the thought of his friend languishing in hell for all eternity. Luke leveraged his one and only life to help his friend see the wisdom and hope of choosing to follow Jesus as Lord.

I love the way Luke climaxes his first book for Theophilus. Everything he writes through 24 chapters climaxes with a personal plea from the Lord of life Himself, *"'The Messiah must suffer and die and rise again on the third day...this message of salvation....There is forgiveness of sins for all who turn to Me!'"* (Luke 24:46,47 LB)

Just as Theophilus was placed purposefully in Luke's life that he might come to know Jesus through Luke, so the Lord has strategically arranged for you to have friends and family with whom you are to share the love and life of Jesus. It's what desperados do.

THE DESPERADO DAILY

Ponder:

"We are Christ's ambassadors; God is making His appeal through us. We speak for Christ when we plead, 'Come back to God.'" (II Corinthians 5:20 NLT)

Practice:

Make a list of family, friends, neighbors and co-workers you'd love to see come to know the Lord of life.

Pray:

"Dear Lord, I am so grateful for all You have done in my life. You have freely forgiven my sins, cleansed me of all guilt and shame, filled me with Your Holy Spirit. I have an abundance of joy, hope, peace and wisdom all because of You. You have made me the target of Your goodness, mercy and grace. Please help me to see the people You have placed in my life as You see them. Help me to love them as You love them. Wield me as Your ambassador to draw them to Your love. In Your name, Amen."

DESPERADO

DAY 18

The DNA of Jesus

THERE'S ONE MORE important issue to address before we get to our Jesus story. From beginning to end, all that Luke writes for Theophilus is intentionally injected with the essential DNA of the church of Jesus. Our Lord made a bold proclamation:

"I will build My church, and all the powers of hell will not prevail against it!" (Matt. 16:18 LB)

I believe every Christ-follower and every local church can embody the hell-conquering power of Jesus if there is a commitment to embrace four deeply-held values. This has become the heart-beat of our church. This is what we believe it means to follow Jesus.

First, Luke did everything he did — all his investigation, every interview, the entirety of his writing — just to bring one person to Jesus. Luke knew this was the priority of all Christ-followers. Luke knew that a guy named Philip invited his friend, Nathaniel, to Jesus by simply saying, "Come and see!" Luke knew, *"The first thing Andrew did was find his brother...And he brought him to Jesus."* (John 1:41,42)

At the church I serve, that's the first item on our agenda when we decide to follow Jesus, the Lord of life. **WE BRING!** We invite our friends and family, "Come and see!"

Second, Luke keeps a strong focus on the all-inclusive nature of Jesus. He highlights how Jesus unconditionally welcomed and accepted everyone: the rich, the poor, the educated, the illiterate, the healthy, the diseased, all races. Luke places special emphasis on how Jesus honored, respected and elevated women

This is at the core of all we do at our church. We create an atmosphere of unconditional acceptance, where everyone belongs — all colors, all cultures, all peoples. Following Jesus means **WE BELONG** and we help others feel they belong.

Imagine how long it took to do all of this extensive investigation and research: Cross-checking all the facts, personally interviewing eyewitnesses, revisiting place after place where Jesus did ministry. All this time — all this effort — was to serve one man, Theophilus. Even more, God gave Luke's willingness to serve a miraculous major ripple effect, so that billions now have been well-served by what Luke did for one person.

That's us. **WE SERVE!** That's what desperados for Jesus do. We serve children. We serve the hungry and the hurting. We serve the single and the married. We serve the addicted and the down-and-out — the grieving, the abused, the divorced. We serve.

But did you catch the last phrase Luke wrote in his introduction? Everything Luke did was to help Theophilus grow *"So that you may know the certainty of the things you have been taught."* (Luke 1:4 NIV) All this was done to help one man grow in Christ.

And that's us. **WE GROW!** It's why we are engaged in worship every weekend. It's why we give ourselves to a study of God's Word. It's why we are devoted to praying for and with each other. It's why we are desperados, we grow in Christ.

Now we are ready for the Jesus story.

"Soon afterward, Jesus went to a town called Nain, and his disciples and a large crowd went along with him. As he approached the town gate, a dead person was being carried out — the only son of his mother, and she was a widow. And a large crowd from the town was with her. When the Lord saw her, his heart went out to her and he said, "Don't cry." Then he went up and touched the bier they were carrying him on, and the bearers stood still. He said, "Young man, I say to you, get up!" The dead man sat up and began to talk, and Jesus gave him back to his mother. They were all filled with awe and praised God. "A great prophet has appeared among us," they said. "God has come to help his people." This news about Jesus spread throughout Judea and the sur-rounding country." (Luke 7:11-17 NIV)

Our story opens with Jesus headed for holy ground. The region around Nain is famous. 800 years earlier, the great prophet Elisha raised a boy from the dead in this same area. It took incredible effort and a ton of prayer, but the miracle happened.

Jesus travels to Nain to give irrefutable evidence that He is greater than any prophet, He is God. Everything in Luke's historical record is meant to offer conclusive proof that Jesus is Lord. This is what He wants to teach the crowd that follows Him.

In fact, on one level, this is the story of two crowds. One crowd has decided to follow the Lord of life. They are energized, excited, full of hopeful anticipation. What will Jesus do to blow their minds today? They are driven by enthusiastic expectation. Jesus always has a way of teaching that instills joy, elevates hope, provokes grateful worship and increases their love for God. This crowd is following the Lord of life. It is what desperados do.

The other crowd is following the lord of death. The crowd exiting Nain on their way to the cemetery is helpless, full of despair. Inner anguish consumes them — agonizing emotions, no hope, no peace, no joy. So it is for all those who follow the lord of death.

Two crowds headed for the same cemetery — one is filled with anxiety and dark despair; the other is filled with joy and hopeful anticipation. The actual difference between the two crowds is who they follow — the Lord of life or the lord of death. Which crowd are you in?

This story is mostly about the two leaders. Jesus, the Lord of life, is leading a mission. Leading the other crowd, the widow is a miserable mess, following the lord of death. Follow the lord of death and you'll always be a miserable mess — depressed, despairing. Follow Jesus, and the joy of the Lord of life will always be your strength. Jesus, the Lord of life, always knows exactly what He will do for those who follow Him. The widow, leading the funeral procession, has no idea what she will do next. In the darkness of despair, all she can do is put one foot in front of the other on her way to the cemetery.

The whole point of this story is to provoke each of us to ask, who am I following with my one and only life, the Lord of life or the lord of death?

THE DESPERADO DAILY

Ponder:

> "I will build My church; and all the powers of hell shall not prevail against it!" (Matthew 16:18 LB)

Practice:

> Bear the DNA of Jesus — bring, belong, serve and grow!

Pray:

> "Dear Jesus, I praise You as the Lord of life. Following You is my biggest joy and my biggest challenge. Please forgive me when I neglect to pursue You with all my heart. Please recalibrate my priorities. I want to aim my life at bringing, belonging, serving and growing. Thank You for aiming Your love at me. In Your name, Amen."

DESPERADO
DAY 19

Holy Happenings
with a Relentless Lord

EVERYTHING JESUS DOES is strategically designed to move us to follow Him as the Lord of life. In our story Jesus takes five specific actions to challenge us to be His desperados.

First, we see that **Jesus travels!** Jesus is El Roi, the God who sees. He knows the exact moment in which the despairing widow will lead her grieving crowd out of Nain.

Jesus knows how she hates the thought of walking this path of pain again. She has already buried a husband. How can she go on living without her only son?

Jesus has 25 miles to cover before the sun starts to set in the west. He's up and out early. If Jesus is up, His desperados are up. If Jesus is on the move, His desperados move with Him. As they travel across the 25 miles, they attract a growing crowd of followers. There's nothing like walking in the wake of the Lord of life as He makes

His way to where He is going to work His wonders. Jesus is always up to something great.

This is good news for us. Jesus was willing to exhaust Himself to get to this nobody of a widow. This helps us understand that the Lord of life will cross any difficult distance to get to us when our lives are fractured into a plethora of painful pieces.

Jesus sees you. He knows what you're going through. The Lord of life comes to you. The question is: will you follow Him or will you keep trailing after the lord of death?

We also must remember that Jesus is a rabbi, which means **He teaches**. As a rabbi, Jesus, the Lord of life, teaches His followers by taking them not to a classroom, but on a field trip of faith. He wants them to know that when they choose to follow Him, He leads them to the miraculous.

Great things have been done by great men in this specific area where Jesus is taking His followers. Jesus is teaching them that He is greater than any great man. The whole point of this field trip is to show them that Jesus is God, the Lord of life.

So, what if Jesus is God? What is God really like? What does God do? These questions are at the heart of what Jesus is teaching. Check it out. *"As Jesus approached the town gate, a dead person was being carried out..."* (Luke 7:12 NIV)

The dead person would be wrapped in white linen burial cloth and placed on wooden planks carried by what we would call pallbearers. Jesus had planned this sacred moment with perfect timing, so those who followed the Lord of life and those who followed the lord of death would collide at this precise spot.

For Jesus' teaching, it is deeply significant whom this dead person is *"...the only son of his mother...."* The Greek word here for "only son" is "monogenes." It's the very same Greek word used of Jesus in John 3:16: *"For God so loved the world that He gave His ONE AND ONLY SON, that whoever believes in Him will not die, but have eternal life!"* (John 3:16 NIV)

Jesus would exert His power over death to raise this one and only son of the widow to point to His own personal victory over death in His Easter morning resurrection. Jesus is the Lord of life. Death cannot hold Him. When we choose to follow the Lord of life, His victory over death is our victory over death. We follow Him right through the dark valley of shadow. If Jesus can take us through death, He can take us through anything.

So Jesus does more than travel to us in our time of need — **Jesus teaches!** His life lessons are always meant to point us to the fact that He, as God, is greater than anything, even death itself. When we follow Him, we follow Him all the way to heaven.

This life lesson is about what Jesus brings when He comes and teaches. Check it out. "When the Lord saw her, He had compassion on her and said to her, 'Do not weep.'" (Luke 7:13 RSV) The phrase "do not weep" basically means, "You do not have to weep." "You're weeping, but you don't have to." Why? The Lord of life sees you. The Lord of life comes to you. The Lord of life brings His compassion to you.

The Greek word used here for compassion is "splagchna." **"Splagchna" is an inner passion that takes sacrificial action for the good of others.**

If there is one word that most captures what Jesus brings when He comes to you, it is "splagchna." This is how deeply Jesus feels about you and whatever struggle you're going through. He does more than feel it. He takes sacrificial action to your good.

This is what the work of Christ on the cross is all about. He sees how damaged we are by our own sin and shame. He takes sacrificial action in our behalf and to our good. He dies, so we can live. He is our Substitute, taking the punishment we deserve, so we go free. He is made filthy with our sin, so we can be cleansed of all guilt and shame.

Jesus is compassion itself. The compassion of Jesus means **He touches!** In our story, He steps by the stunned widow and touches the coffin.

God wants us to do more than read this story. He wants us to see ourselves in it. Out of His great compassion, Jesus longs to touch whatever has gone dead in our lives, whatever has gone dead in our relationships; whatever has gone dead in our emotions, whatever has gone dead in our faith.

Jesus is right here, right now in the air we breathe, and He wants to touch every dead place in our lives. At the very same time Jesus touches us, He speaks to us. That's exactly what happened in our story. At the very same time He touched the dead man, He spoke to the dead man. *"Young man, I say to you, get up!"* (Luke 7:14 NIV)

When Elisha raised a boy from the dead near this same spot, it was all struggle, pray, struggle, pray and keep struggling and keep praying. Finally the boy was raised. But Jesus just says two words, "Get up." Jesus is God, so when He spoke, *"The dead man sat up and began to talk!"* (Luke 7:15 NIV)

You'd think all the pallbearers would have flopped over in a faint. I wonder what the young man felt, when a surging rush of supernatural, resurrection power recharged his dead body with life. His first breath was filled with words. I wonder what he said. Was he saying, "Thank You"? Was he praising God? Was he calling for his mother?

Can you imagine that moment? Can you imagine what that mom felt when she held the warm body of her son in her arms again? Did she ever stop kissing him? Maybe she stripped off the grave clothes and cried out, "Bring my son a fine robe. He's alive!"

What was a downer of a funeral becomes a blow-out fun celebration. This is the thing about Jesus. **Jesus transforms!**

Now the two crowds were one crowd. They all were transformed. *"They all realized they were in a place of holy mystery, that God was at work among them. They were quietly worshipful and noisily grateful...They said, 'God has come to help His people!'"* (Luke 7:16 MSG, NIV)

It's the wild possibility of holy happenings like this that keeps desperados in passionate pursuit of Jesus, the relentless Lord of life.

THE DESPERADO DAILY

Ponder:

> "For God so loved the world that He gave His one and only Son, that whoever believes in Him shall not perish but have eternal life." (John 3:16 NIV)

Practice:

> Be the compassion of Jesus. Today take sacrificial action for the good of someone God has placed on the path of your life.

Pray:

> "Dear Jesus, Your compassion moves You to come to me in my need. Thank You for letting nothing stop You from helping me. In my struggle, teach me what I need to learn about your Lordship. Touch my life with Your power. I want to be transformed by Your relentless love. You are my help, my hope. I praise You. In Your name, Amen."

DESPERADO

DAY 20

Transforming Power of Perspective

ARE YOU A positive "glass is half-full" kind of person? Or do you look more on the negative side, as a "glass is half-empty" kind of person? Does it really matter? Do you go through life wearing rose-colored glasses so everything looks really good? Or are you more apt to live under a dark cloud, making it hard to see anything in a good light? What is your perspective on life? And again, does it really matter?

Are you kidding me? Your perspective on life determines everything about your life.

Obviously your perspective has no control over what happens to you, but your perspective gives you full control over how you handle what happens to you. Your perspective is what happens **IN** you. Your perspective on life fully determines how you think, how you feel and what you do. **Your perspective on life will lift you up or drag you down!**

If you have a pessimistic perspective, you see your troubles as big problems, excuses for why nothing ever works out for you. You see yourself as a victim of life's unfairness.

If you have an optimistic perspective, you think life is good, getting better all the time. You see your troubles as big possibilities — stepping stones to big victories.

Do you have a rose-colored perspective or a dark cloud perspective? Are you an optimist or a pessimist? Maybe you say, "I'm not an optimist or a pessimist. I'm a realist. I see life for what it is."

I have one question for you: are you a spiritual desperado, recklessly pursuing a relentless Jesus? If you have fully surrendered your life to Jesus, you can be the ultimate optimist. Here's your best, boundless reality as a follower of Jesus:

> *"I can do all things through Christ, who strengthens me!"* (Philippians 4:13)

> *"God is able to do immeasurably more than all we ask or imagine, according to His power that is at work within us."* (Ephesians 3:20)

> *"We know that in all things God works for the good of those who love Him!"* (Romans 8:28)

> *"In all these things we are more than conquerors through Him who loved us!"* (Romans 8:37)

Sometimes I will pointedly ask people, "Don't you ever get sick of living under a dark cloud? Or do you simply love the dark drama you create for yourself and others?"

If you find your life severely hampered and your relationships hurting by your negative perspective, you don't have to live that way a moment longer. You can change your life by changing your perspective. It will not be necessarily easy. But the hard work is worth the huge win, as your life and relationships are elevated, enhanced and enriched by the supernatural favor of God at work to your good.

One of the most profound aspects of your perspective on life is that you can change it. You can get a new life by getting a new perspective. You can change the way you think and feel. You don't have to be overwhelmed a minute longer. You can overcome. You don't have to just survive. You can thrive. You don't have to cope. You can conquer. If you're tired of being a victim, living in the dumps under a dark cloud, you can change your perspective on life. Jesus will lift you up on the higher ground of abundant living.

You get the best perspective on life by passionately pursuing your relentless Jesus to see and experience life from His perspective! Then you can shout out with the psalmist, David: *"My cup overflows!"* (Psalm 23:5) Then you can experience all that Jesus has designed and destined for your life. *"I came that they may have life, and have it abundantly!"* (John 10:10)

Do you see the comma in the middle of that sentence? Which side of the comma are you living on? Are you just getting by in life or are you doing life more abundantly?

Here's how you get the abundant perspective of Jesus on your life:

Focus on whatever is good in your life.

Jesus puts good in every life. And Jesus puts something good in anything bad that happens in life. Find the good. Celebrate the good and put all your focus on it.

"Whatever is true, whatever is noble, whatever is right, whatever is pure, whatever is lovely, whatever is admirable — if anything is excellent or praiseworthy — think about such things." (Philippians 4:8 NIV)

Focus on being thankful. An attitude of gratitude has the power to transform your life.

"Don't worry about anything; instead, pray about everything. Tell God what you need and thank Him for all He has done. Then you will experience God's peace, which exceeds anything we can understand. His peace will guard your hearts and minds, as you live in Christ Jesus!" (Phil. 4:6,7 NLT)

Find someone to serve! This is the secret of having a "blessed life" perspective.

This is how Jesus did life and promised:

"I've laid down a pattern (of service) for you. What I've done, you do...and live a blessed life!" (John 13:15,17 MSG)

Find Jesus! When you passionately pursue your relentless Jesus, your journey is filled with great joy. The joy of the Lord becomes the sustaining power of your life. *"For the joy of the LORD is your strength!"* (Nehemiah 8:10 NIV)

Desperados see the relentless love of Jesus at work in all of life!

THE DESPERADO DAILY

Ponder:

> "Whatever is true; whatever is noble; whatever is right; whatever is pure; whatever is lovely; whatever is admirable — if anything is excellent or praiseworthy — think about such things." (Philippians 4:8 NIV)

Practice:

> Focus on whatever is good. Focus on being thankful. Focus on serving others and finding Jesus at work to your good in all of life.

Pray:

> "Dear Lord Jesus, please give me Your perspective on life. Sharpen my focus on what truly matters — loving God and other people. I want Your joy to be my sustaining strength. Thank You for giving me a life overflowing with good. In Your name, Amen."

DESPERADO

DAY 21

Looking Into the Face of Jesus

To HELP YOU get a Jesus perspective on life, I want to take you into a Jesus story which opens: *"On a Sabbath…"* (Luke 13:10 NIV)

Let me give you a crash course on the Sabbath. The Sabbath is the most important of all Jewish holidays. And it happens every Saturday. Isn't that wild! Actually it begins each Friday evening at sunset and ends every Saturday evening at sunset.

Maybe you think, "Whoever came up with the idea of having a holiday every Saturday?"

It was all God's plan right from the start of things. In the beginning there was nothing — absolutely nothing but empty darkness. On day one of history God goes to work. He starts creating. On day two God keeps creating. On day three God creates some more. On day four God's on a roll. He puts on a creative cosmic light show. With days five and six of creation, it's all a done deal —

the heavens with solar systems, universes and galaxies; the earth, the sky, the sea; all filled with creeping, crawling, swimming and flying creatures.

At the center of it all was a glorious garden. In the midst of the garden was God's masterpiece — man and woman. God made everything out of nothing in six days.

The Bible says:

"Then God blessed the seventh day and made it holy, because on it He rested from all the work of creating that He had done." (Genesis 2:3 NIV)

God did not rest because He was tired. God took a break from work to focus solely on His relationship with man and woman. The humans also took a break from their work to focus solely on their relationship with God. Do you know how they did that? First, they worshipped God. Second, they brought Him offerings to thank Him for His goodness. They talked to God in prayer. And they listened and learned as God spoke His Word into their lives.

So do you know what the whole point was for the Sabbath — this God-blessed day to worship and bring offerings and pray and listen to God's Word? The whole point was to set aside the time to get a new perspective on life — to get God's perspective on life.

That's why we gather at church each weekend — to worship, to bring our offerings, to pray and hear God's Word. We gather to get God's perspective on life. That's why it is so important to be present and fully engaged in worship every weekend. When we miss worship, we lose God's perspective on life.

I have to tell you something. There was one more essential part of Sabbath worship in the day of Jesus. It was called "tzedakah" which means "**offering for the poor.**" The people had already given their tithes — 10% of their regular income. The offering for the poor was a little extra — a few dollars extra. This offering for the poor had special intent. The purpose of this extra offering is captured in the Hebrew phrase "**tikkun olam**" which means "**to repair the world.**"

In the day of Jesus, part of Sabbath celebration was giving a little more to fix what is broken in the world. This was an exciting discovery for me, because at our church we do the very same thing every weekend. We call it our Dollar Club. As we leave church, we drop a few extra dollars in our Dollar Club buckets. Each Wednesday those dollars are distributed to some person or family who has suffered a significant loss. It's our way of doing "tikkun olam", helping to repair what is broken in our world.

Let's get on with our Jesus story. *"On a Sabbath Jesus was teaching in one of the synagogues."* (Luke 13:10 NIV) Synagogues were places of community worship.

Luke does not tell us here exactly what Jesus was teaching. This is the tenth and final instance of Jesus teaching God's Word on the Sabbath in a synagogue. We know for sure what Jesus said the very first time He taught in a synagogue on the Sabbath. We know because Luke tells us. *"Unrolling the scroll, Jesus found the place where it was written: 'God's Spirit is on Me; He has chosen Me to preach the message of good news to the poor; sent Me to announce pardon to the prisoners, recovery of sight to the blind; to set the burdened and battered free; to announce, 'This is God's time to act!'"* (Luke 4:18,19 MSG)

I wonder if at the very moment He reads the words: *"to set the burdened and battered free; to announce: 'This is*

God's time to act!'" — a woman tries to sneak unnoticed into the room.

She does not want to be seen because she is unsightly. She has an ugly disfigurement and disability. Her spine is rigidly bent over, so that she cannot stand erect. Can you imagine her perspective on life? Wherever she goes, she goes all bent over. So she can't go fast. It's awkward. She has to be careful. Whatever she does, she has to do it all bent over — getting dressed, bathing, taking her meals, going to the market, getting back into bed at night. It had to be very painful in private and embarrassing in public. Wherever she goes, all she can see are other people's dirty feet. What a perspective.

She comes a little late, trying not to be seen. She wants to be there without being humiliated. But there's no sneaking by Jesus, particularly if you are a person in pain.

> *"When Jesus saw her, He called her forward and said to her, 'Woman, you are set free from your infirmity.' Then He put His hands on her, and immediately she straightened up and praised God." (Luke 13:12,13 NIV)*

Now she has a new perspective on life. Now she's looking into the face of Jesus. That's where we all want to get. That's why we recklessly pursue our relentless Jesus. We want Him to give us His perspective on life. We want to see life as He sees it.

It can happen as we engage in weekend worship. This woman didn't ask to be healed. Jesus took all the initiative because she was desperate to worship a good God through her gross pain, to be in the presence of Jesus and pursue His relentless love.

THE DESPERADO DAILY

Ponder:

"God's Spirit is on Me; He's chosen Me to preach the Message of good news to the poor. Sent Me to announce pardon to prisoners and recovery of sight to the blind. To set the burdened and battered free; to announce, 'This is God's time to act.'" (Luke 4:18,19 MSG)

Practice:

Be desperate to worship a good God through any painful impossibility, to be in the presence of Jesus, recklessly pursuing His relentless love.

Pray:

"Dear Jesus, let Your Spirit be on me. You've chosen me to be a bearer of good news to the poor. Use me to serve the burdened and battered. O Lord, take action for a hurting world through me. I am so grateful to be loved by You. In Your name, Amen."

DESPERADO
DAY 22

That's Not Fair!

LIFE IS ABSOLUTELY UNFAIR FOR EVERYONE! You know this is the unfortunate truth. You know from personal experience. Life is not fair for anyone. Do you know what feels very unfair about life? Bad things happen to good people. The worst thing can happen to the best person. It's not fair. Do you know what feels the most unfair about life? Good things that happen to bad people. That's not fair.

You know what I mean. You're a good person. You're certainly not a terrible person. You and your spouse just want to get pregnant. Is that too much to ask? You try everything, but you don't get a baby. You read in the paper about people who have been blessed with children, but they neglect, mistreat or abuse their kids. What's up with that? That's not fair.

Your wife is the best. She is loving — so giving, so devoted to family, so thoughtless of self and willing to sacrifice for others. Yet she's the one with stage four cancer. Not fair.

Or your husband — he's such a good man. He's hard working on the job and at home. He is everything to his family. He loves you. He's the best dad. He's always there for you and your children. All the neighbors know that he'd do anything for anyone any time. But when there are layoffs at work, he's the first to be let go. It is so unfair.

You're a good person and bad things happen to you. It hurts when you look around only to see other people getting good breaks and you get squat. Life is so unfair.

Here's a question I bet you've thought a number of times. Where is God when life is unfair? What is God doing when we suffer unfairly? Here's what I want you to know:

When we suffer unfairly, God does His best to draw us to Jesus!

Jesus explained how this works. *"The Father, who sent Me, is in charge. He draws people to Me — that's the only way you'll ever come. Only then do I do My work, putting people together, setting them back on their feet."* (John 6:44 MSG)

Maybe this is the more important question. **When life is unfair, what are we doing to free up Jesus to work miraculously to our good?**

Here's the deal. God takes His responsibility to us very seriously. He will always hold up His end of the relationship. When life treats us unfairly, God does everything He can to draw us to Jesus. What we do when God gets us to Jesus, that's on us. Do we listen to Him or do we ignore Him? Do we follow Him or do we keep going our own way, doing our own thing? Do we fight Him or do we free up Jesus to work miraculously to our good? We get to choose. When we choose right, Jesus does more than make things right. By His relentless love, He keeps pouring on His miraculous help and hope.

Let me explain by taking you into a Jesus story. To set the story up let me give you a mental image of what is taking place. There are two groups of people, separated by a great distance. It will take time, but these two groups are on a collision course with each other. Life has been cruelly unfair, but God is drawing hurting people to Jesus.

One group knows exactly where they are going, because they are being led by Jesus. This group is actually a large crowd. But out front are twelve point men. In Hebrew the number twelve carries great significance. **Twelve symbolizes spiritual authority.**

These twelve leading men are led by the one and only Jesus. In Hebrew the number **one symbolizes absolute uniqueness!** That's our Jesus. *"For God so loved the world, He gave His ONE AND ONLY Son!"* (John 3:16 NIV)

That's one side of the scene. This group of twelve, led by the one and only Jesus, has God's authority to fix the unfairness of life and work everything together for the good.

The other group has no idea where they're going; together they're just trying to find Jesus. Life has been hurtfully unfair and unkind to this group. It's a small group of ten men. But in Hebrew ten is significant. **Ten symbolizes human harmony — unity.**

These ten men all share the same purpose and passion. All they care about is getting to Jesus together. It has to be together. In the day of Jesus, a group of ten Jewish men was called a **"minyan"**. It was believed that when you had a minyan — ten men united together with one purpose in worship, prayer and the study of God's Word — then God Himself would show up to guide you, to help you and to bless you miraculously.

In fact, there was one blessing of God that could only be experienced when you had ten men united together in a minyan. You needed ten men to experience the following blessing: *"The LORD bless you and keep you; the LORD make His face shine on you and be gracious to you; the LORD turn His face toward you and give you peace (and make you prosper)."* (Numbers 6:24-26 NIV, MSG)

So here's the answer to one of our questions. What must we do to free up Jesus to work miraculously to our good? **When life is terribly unfair, we position ourselves to receive God's unbelievable blessing by coming together with others in united worship, united prayer and united devotion to hear God's Word.** This is what we give our lives to with others to free Jesus up to work miraculously to our good.

THE DESPERADO DAILY

....

Ponder:

> "The Father who sent Me is in charge. He draws people to Me — that's the only way you'll ever come. Only then do I do my work, putting people together, setting them on their feet..." (John 6:44 MSG)

Practice:

> Position yourself to receive God's unbelievable blessing by coming together with others in united worship, united prayer and united devotion to hear God's Word.

Pray:

> "Dear Heavenly Father, please draw me to Jesus. I so desperately need Him to do His work in my life. I will free His hand to do the miraculous by joining His church in united worship, prayer and the study of His Word. Thank You, Lord, for always doing Your part. I will do my part. Please shine Your face on me. In Jesus' name, Amen."

DESPERADO

DAY 23

The Freeing Power of Obedience

WHAT BOUND THESE ten men together in reckless pursuit of Jesus was the unspeakable bad thing that had unfairly happened to each of them. All ten men were lepers.

Leprosy is like a cancer on the outside of the body, eating up the skin and destroying nerve endings. It usually started somewhere on the face — the nose, an ear, the chin or on a cheek. Then it spread like a grotesque tumor, ravaging every piece of skin it touched; penetrating the teeth and attacking the throat, so that a leper had only a weak, raspy voice. Extremities, like fingers and hands, feet and toes, would just die and fall off. Ultimately, this hideous disease would attack the leper's internal organs.

Leprosy was easily transmitted by one's breath or body contact, so lepers were worse than social outcasts. They were absolutely isolated outside the walls of the city, usually living in the town trash heap, trying to survive by scrounging through garbage for anything edible. Lepers were believed to be cursed by God. It was totally unfair. It was just their terrible misfortune to have contracted the bacteria that caused the disease.

If a leper saw you coming in their direction, it was their responsibility to cry out as loud as their damaged throats would allow them, "Unclean. Unclean, unclean," so you could avoid them at all costs.

> *"It happened that as Jesus made His way toward Jeru-salem, He crossed over the border between Samaria and Galilee. As He approached a village, ten men, all lepers, met Him. They kept their distance, but raised their voices, calling out: 'Jesus, Master, have mercy on us!' (Luke 17:11-13 MSG)*

Two things jump out here as prerequisites for having Jesus work miraculously to your good. **Honor Jesus and humble yourself!**

The word "Master" is an acknowledgement that the person addressed carries the authority to do the miraculous. Then they humbly cry out for mercy. This is like a spiritual one-two punch that sets you up to be the target of Jesus' miraculous goodness.

Honor Jesus and humble yourself, so Jesus is free to go to work to your good.

Something else incredibly significant is happening here. Did you notice that the lepers did not cry, "Unclean, unclean"? Now that they had met Jesus, their identity was not tied to how bad life had been to them. They anchored their new identity to how good Jesus would be to them.

Here's what happened. **"When Jesus saw them, He said, 'Go, show yourselves to the priest.' And as they went, they were cleansed."** (Luke 17:14 NIV)

Here's an important insight most people miss. You can honor Jesus until you're blue in the face, humble yourself all day long; but that is all just hot air unless you're willing to obey Jesus. It was as they took action — "as they went" — that they got their miracle.

Let's make this personal. Let's say you suffer some unfair financial setback. You know you need the Master's help. You humble yourself and admit your desperate need, but nothing happens. You honor Jesus, confessing Him as your Lord, but nothing happens. You complain, "What's up, Jesus?" Jesus says, "What's up with you? It's when you obey My Word with your finances, bringing ten percent of your income into My House out of every pay period that I open the floodgates of heaven and pour out more blessing than you have room enough to hold."

This is the way Jesus is free to work in all areas of our life — our marriage, our emotions, our career, our friendships. **Obedience frees Jesus to do the miraculous.**

In our Jesus story, the ten lepers, now cleansed of their deadly disease, were making a bee-line to a priest. They knew there was a spiritual process they must submit to in order to be declared clean and allowed back with their families. When the priest saw that the lepers were miraculously healed, he would provide two pigeons for each leper. One pigeon would die for the leper. The pigeon's blood would be placed on the leper's ear lobe, and the leper would promise to listen to God. Blood would be placed on the leper's thumb. The leper would promise to always do what God said to do. Blood was placed on his big toe. Now the leper would always follow the Lord. The second pigeon was released as a sign that the disease was gone and would never return.

If this was the end of the story, it's a good story. It's especially good because it is a picture of the work of Christ on the cross in our behalf. His blood would be shed and applied to our lives. As desperados, we listen to our Lord, do what our Lord says to do, go where our Lord sends us. Our diseased souls are cleansed of all guilt and shame. The punishment for our sins is taken completely away, never to return.

> "One of the lepers, when he realized that he was healed, turned around and came back, shouting his gratitude, glorifying God. He kneeled at Jesus' feet, so grateful. He couldn't thank Jesus enough — and he was a Samaritan. Jesus said, 'Were not ten healed? Where are the nine? Can none be found to come back and give glory to God except this outsider?' Then He said to him, 'Get up. On your way. Your faith has healed and saved you!'" (Luke 17:15-19 MSG)

On the basis of his thankful heart, this man gets more than healed. He gets saved. He gets more than a temporary blessing. He gets an eternal reward. This is the relentless love of Jesus. He always gives better and more to those who express their gratitude in heart-felt worship. Jesus digs deeper and distributes more to the deeply appreciative.

THE DESPERADO DAILY

Ponder:

"Not everyone who says to Me, 'Lord, Lord,' will enter the kingdom of heaven, but only the one WHO DOES the will of My Father who is in heaven." (Matt. 7:21 NIV)

Practice:

Free Jesus to do the miraculous by obeying Him fully and thanking Him freely.

Pray:

"Lord Jesus, You've been better to me than I could ever deserve. Thank You for Your grace. I also thank You that Your mercy protects me from the consequences I do deserve. I even thank You for the painful times. The Father uses them to draw me to You. You never fail to be my help and my hope. I love you. In Your name, Amen."

DESPERADO
DAY 24

To Destroy the Work of the Devil

HAVE YOU EVER been hurt by a lie? Someone said something viciously untrue about you. And it hurt. Or you were even more hurt when you found out that some-one you trusted had lied straight to your face. That was extremely hurtful.

I remember the first time I got caught in a lie. I'm sure it was not the first time I lied. It was just the first time I got caught. I was in elementary school when I lied to my mom. Within a matter of hours, she learned that what I'd told her was an out-and-out lie. She sent me to my bedroom to wait for my dad to get home from work. When my dad came into my room, I was in bed, lying on my stomach. He asked me if I had lied. I said, "Yes." He spanked my bottom right where I lay. He cried while he did it and I cried too. The spanking hurt, but what hurt more was knowing that my lie had hurt my dad.

That's the way lies work. We've all been lied about. We've all been lied to. And we've all lied. Lies hurt us.

Our lies hurt others. Lies always hurt more and longer than we ever thought they would. **So why do we lie?**

To answer that question let me ask another. **What are the most hurtful lies?** The most damning and damaging lies are the lies we believe told to us by Satan.

I hope you believe that Satan is real. All the evidence I need for the existence of Satan is that Jesus believed in the existence of Satan. And Jesus warned us of Satan's lies.

To an angry mob, wanting to kill Him, Jesus says, *"You belong to your father, the devil, and you want to carry out your father's desires. He was a murderer from the beginning, not holding to the truth, for there is no truth in him. When he lies, he speaks his native language, for he is a liar and the father of lies."* (John 8:44)

Satan is by his very nature a liar — an habitual liar, a compulsive liar. Thus, Jesus calls Satan the father of all lies. When we lie, Satan is lying through us. It hurts us. It hurts the people we lie about. It hurts the people we lie to. It hurts the heart of God.

What is most hurtful is when we believe the lies Satan tells us. Satan lies to us to deceive us. Satan wants to deceive us so he can destroy us — destroy our families, destroy our friendships, destroy our faith, destroy our finances. Satan is out to destroy God's dream for our lives.

The name **Satan means adversary**. Satan is your most dangerous and deadly foe. He is the arch adversary of God and our Lord, Jesus. Satan is the arch adversary of the Holy Spirit and the Holy Scriptures. Satan is the arch adversary of the church. Satan is my worst adversary. Satan is your worst adversary.

Here's how Satan works. Satan lies to us to mess with our minds and our emotions. If we believe his lies, our minds fill with worry. The more we believe, the more we worry. Satan lies to us to make us afraid. The more we believe his lies, the more fear we feel. If we believe Satan's lies, we get angry. The more we believe, the angrier we get.

Everyone worries. Everyone feels anxiety and becomes afraid. Everyone gets angry. We all have emotions and it's healthy to have them. But when we get stuck in the negativity and hurtfulness of the emotion, that's when Satan pours on the lies.

Here's the wisdom of God's Word. *"In your anger do not sin. Do not let the sun go down while you are still angry; and do not give the devil a foothold."* (Eph. 4:26)

The word here for "foothold" means "a place of opportunity." What Paul says about anger is also true of fear or worry or any negative emotion. Don't hold on to it. If you don't let go of the fear, anger or worry, you give that lying devil more opportunity to mess up your mind and emotions — more opportunity to deceive and destroy.

Here's the good news. **We can defeat Satan's lies with God's truth!**

Here's a Triumphant Truism: *"The reason the Son of God appeared was to destroy the devil's work!"* (I John 3:8 NIV)

I pray this triumphant truth every day. I ask Jesus to destroy the devil's work in my life — completely obliterate it. I call each of my family members' names before the Lord and pray for Him to destroy the devil's work in my family. I pray for the devil's work to be destroyed in my staff, crying out for a wondrous harmony among us. I ask Jesus to destroy the devil's work in His church. It's a prayer for Him to protect our unity of faith, hope and love. Finally, I remind the Lord that tens of thousands of people in our region are living in spiritual darkness and in bondage to sin. I pray for every heart in every home to find true freedom by coming into the light of God's saving love through a real relationship with Jesus. I want to cover all the bases in the destruction of Satan's work.

Here's another *Triumphant Truism: "There is Someone in your hearts who is stronger than any evil...in this wicked world."* (I John 4:4 LB)

Whenever our adversary tries to mess with our minds and emotions, all he can ever do is just blow smoke. He is not strong enough to do anything else. However, we'll choke on his smoke if we try to rely on how smart we are, how rich we are, how holy we are, how anything we are. Our hope of victory in every area of life is secure, because our Jesus within us is greater, stronger, richer, smarter than all the hosts of hell.

Here's another *Triumphant Truism: "You will know the Truth; and the Truth will set you free!"* (John 8:32 NIV)

Think of how free your friendships would be if Satan completely lost any place of opportunity in your friendships. Think of how free your family would be if Satan lost any hold over your family. Think of how free you would be of anger, worry and fear — free to feel joy, hope, love and peace — if Satan lost any place of opportunity in your life.

Jesus is the Truth.

Know Jesus; know freedom. No Jesus; no freedom.

THE DESPERADO DAILY

Ponder:

> "There is Someone in your hearts, who is stronger than any evil...in this wicked world." (I John 4:4 LB)

Practice:

Study God's truth until you can wield it effectively to defeat all the lies of Satan.

Pray:

> "Lord Jesus, please destroy the work of Satan in my life. I hate his lies. As I study Your Word, burn Your great promises in my mind and heart, so I can defeat any satanic effort to deceive and destroy Your dream for my life. In Your name, Amen."

DESPERADO
DAY 25

When Satan Turns
and Runs
the Other Way

I GREW UP in Small Town U.S.A. in the sixties. It was awesome. I loved it. One of my favorite memories is something that happened every summer. Our little community put on a country carnival with carnival rides, carnival food and carnival amusements. But for me the highpoint was the greased pig chase.

For those of you unfamiliar with this form of farm fun, let me explain. A penned area is created with fencing. Young boys pay a quarter each to participate. Loads of grease is slathered all over a small pig. A dozen boys are lined up and the pig is released. Mass chaos erupts. The pig runs around, wildly zig-zagging through boys' legs, like its tail is on fire. The boys (girls are way too smart to get suckered into this) launch their bodies at the little porker, hoping to hold on and win a prize.

I wanted that prize. When a bunch of boys chase the pig in my direction, I go to tackle it like I'm a Green Bay linebacker. I have visions of victory. I get my skinny arms around that chubby belly, squeezing for all I'm worth, but that slimy pig squirts out of my arms. Losing my grip, I fall on my face, defeated and smeared up as greasy as the pig. Rats.

Let my goofy, greased pig memory from over fifty years ago serve as our metaphor. The evil one, our adversary, is ever at work to put the grab on our heads and our hearts. What if we were so slick Satan has no chance but to lose his grip and fall on his face?

To show how it's possible to get Satan to fall away from our lives, let's get into a Jesus story. But first, I want to give you a fresh image of Jesus. This is a Jesus better than you've ever dreamed. Once I describe this Jesus to you, I want this to be how you see Him for the rest of your life. Are you ready?

Please open your mind to a Jesus so full of joy He cannot stand still. He is kicking up his heels. Jesus is so full of energetic joy He cannot contain it. He is bouncing up and down, pumping the air with His fists, shouting, "Yes! Yes! Yes!"

All the while Jesus is surrounded by seventy-two people, all of them full of joy. All seventy-two people carry within them a sense of pure jubilance. Though, honestly, compared to Jesus, they look like a bunch of store mannequins.

Jesus is jumping for joy. Jesus is doing cartwheels. Jesus is running from guy to guy — hugging them, slapping them on the back. Jesus is chest-bumping guys. Jesus grabs guys and starts to dance with them. Next thing they know, Jesus is off dancing by Himself, doing end zone celebrations. Jesus moonwalks. This is how I imagine His joy.

Here's what we know for sure. Finally, Jesus falls to His knees, lifts his arms to the heavens, raises His face and gives a full-throated shout at the top of His lungs, *"I praise You, Father, Lord of Heaven and earth!"* (Luke 10:21 NIV)

Jesus absolutely exhausts Himself with excited, enthusiastic, uncontainable joy. My question is this: What got Jesus so drunk on the joy juice? What got *"Jesus, full of joy through the Holy Spirit!"* (Luke 10:21 NIV)?

We don't have to guess because He tells us Himself. Here's what had happened:

> *"The seventy-two returned with joy and said, 'Lord, even the demons submit to us in Your Name!"* (Luke 10:17 NIV)

These seventy-two guys are so full of joy they forget their manners. They don't say, "Hey, Jesus, how have you been? It's good to see You again." No. They're so excited that they blurt out their joy. "We speak Your powerful, awesome, amazing Name and the devil turns and runs the other way. It's incredible."

Jesus says, "I know. I know, guys. I am so proud of you. I'm so pumped by what God is doing in you and through you. Guys, you have no idea what you've done. *I saw Satan fall like lightning from heaven!"* (Luke 10:18 NIV)

How would you like to see Satan lose his grip and fall away from our nation as fast as lightning? How would you like to see Satan lose his grip and fall away from our schools as fast as lightning? How would you like to see Satan lose his grip and fall away from our church, our campuses and our entire community as fast as lightning?

Let's get personal. How would you like to see Satan lose his grip and fall away from your mind and emotions as fast as lightning? How would you like to see Satan lose his grip and fall away from your friendships, your marriage and your children as fast as lightning? How would you like to see Satan lose his grip on everything and everyone precious to you and plummet as fast as lightning back into the hellish pit from which he came? How'd you like to tell Satan to go to hell?

Evidently, an entire group of seventy-two men did something Jesus had told them to do. They did it just the way Jesus said to do it and received the successful results he had promised. It set off a dynamic, divine domino-effect: they were made so slippery Satan couldn't get a grip on them; their use of Jesus' name helped others get so slick that Satan went into a death-spiral right back into hell; they experienced great joy; Jesus was full of joy through the Holy Spirit; and God the Father received rightful praise.

The seventy-two were desperados. They were "ek ouden". They were nobodies from nowhere. They had nothing but the power of Jesus' name and what Jesus had taught them. But that was everything. Remember what Jesus promised about His special instructions: *"I have told you these things so that you will be filled with My joy. Yes, your joy will overflow."* (John 15:17 NLT)

What the seventy-two learned from Jesus we can learn. What the seventy-two did in Jesus' name we can do. If this is exactly what it means to be a desperado in reckless pursuit of a relentless Jesus and we do it, we get joy and others get free. Jesus gets full of joy in the Holy Spirit. God the Father gets praise. And Satan falls back into hell.

THE DESPERADO DAILY

Ponder:

> "I have told you these things so that you will be filled with My joy. Yes, your joy will overflow." (John 15:17 NLT)

Practice:

Learn to wield the power of Jesus' name and what Jesus taught to be so slick that Satan loses his grip on your life and falls as fast as lightning back into the pit of hell.

Pray:

> "Lord Jesus, You are the source of my joy. I want to be the source of Your joy. When I allow myself to be distracted by stuff that doesn't matter and things that won't last, please re-focus my attention on Your teachings, which are the secret to overflowing joy. I want to do what You want me to do. In the Name above all names, Amen."

Absolute Authority

LIKE PACKER FANS love to see the Bears lose and Bear fans love to see the Packers lose, the Lord Jesus loves to watch Satan lose his deadly grip on precious souls and fall as fast as lightning right back into hell. But in Luke's unique account, Jesus saw more than what Satan lost; he saw what His seventy-two desperados gained. What Jesus tells them then is also His promise for us now. *"I have given you authority to trample on snakes and scorpions and to overcome all the power of the enemy; nothing will harm you."* (Luke 10:19 NIV)

"Snakes and scorpions" is a metaphor for Satan and all his demons. Jesus promises there is nothing this evil enemy can do to harm you. He can lie to you, threaten you, try to scare you and intimidate you. But you have been given the authority of Jesus and nothing will harm you.

That's an incredible promise. It provokes an important question. On what basis did Jesus give these seventy-two desperados the absolute authority to overcome all the power of the enemy? I want to know the answer to that question. I want to wield that authority in my life for my family and my church family. I want the authority of Jesus' name to dominate over any lie the evil one throws my way to destroy God's dream for my life. Why did Jesus give His followers full authority over all the power of the enemy?

To find the answer to this question we go back to the very beginning of this Jesus story. *"The Lord appointed seventy-two others and sent them two by two ahead of Him to every town and place He was about to go."* (Luke 10:1 NIV)

I love the fact that Jesus is not just sending out the twelve Apostles. If that was the case, I would never make the cut. The seventy-two are people like us, desperados. I might not be a Peter, Andrew, James or John. But I could be one of the seventy-two and so could you.

But what explodes at me out of the opening line of this story is that Jesus was sending these desperados to all the places where He planned to go. That's what Jesus wants to do with you and me. Jesus has plans to go to people who are dear to us — our friends and family. Jesus has plans to come to our schools, our neighborhoods and places of work. He wants to touch lives and change hearts. But first Jesus calls us to go ahead of Him, by praying for friends and family; by inviting neighbors and co-workers to our worship celebrations, where He loves to show up and show off. We have the privilege of being sent by Jesus to go ahead of him into the lives of people He wants to save.

The brother of Jesus challenges us:

"Whoever brings the sinner back from wandering will save that person from death and bring about the forgiveness of many sins." (James 5:20 NLT)

The Apostle Paul follows suit:

"It's no light thing to know that we'll all one day stand in that Place of judgment. That's why we work urgently with everyone we meet to get them ready to face God." (II Corinthians 5:11 MSG)

Maybe you're thinking, "That's sounds good in the Bible. I'm not sure how it would work in my reality. If I went to people in my life and said, "Come back to God," they'd likely say, "Go away and don't come back."

This may be why the phrases — "Fear not", "Do not be afraid", and "Do not fear" — appear so regularly throughout the Bible. Here are just two of over 100 instances: *"Do not fear, for I am with you; do not be dismayed for I am your God. I will strengthen you and help you....For I am the LORD, your God, who takes hold of your right hand and says to you, 'Do not fear. I will help you.'"* (Isaiah 41:10,13 NIV)

In a football game, if a team goes into the locker room at half-time down by 17 points, a good coach does not criticize his team. He does not try to convince his team that they are better than their opponent. A good coach gives his team a plan to overcome a 17-point deficit, get back in the game, get a victory, work the plan.

That is precisely what Jesus did for the seventy-two. He gave His desperados a four-step action plan to work as they went ahead of Him.

As a desperado, I want to work this Jesus plan in my personal life. I want to lead our church to implement this plan. I dream about achieving the same results those early Christ-followers experienced. I want the joy of the Lord to be our strength. I want us to exercise authority over the power of the enemy and see Satan fall as fast as lightning. I want to give Jesus reason to be full of joy in the Holy Spirit. I want God to be praised.

For over thirty years, the church I serve has stayed focused on this four-step action plan. We keep it as simple and as practical as it was when Jesus first gave it to his followers.

Step 1: *"When you enter a house, first say, 'Peace to this house!'"* *(Luke 10:5 NIV)*

We say: **Pray down the goodness of God on every heart in every home!** Pray, pray, pray, and never stop praying God's goodness over all our friends and family.

Step 2: *"Stay in that house, eating and drinking..."* *(Luke 10:7 NIV)*

In other words: **Build relationships by building into people's lives.** This is such a huge challenge. But the whole process breaks down if we're not willing to intentionally connect more deeply with the people God has placed in our lives.

Step 3: *"Heal the sick who are there!"* *(Luke 10:9 NIV)*

The Lord opens windows of insight into our relationships with those who need His love. He enables us to see into lives and meet needs, even if it takes a miracle. This is everything, because it sets the stage for the most important thing.

Step 4: *"Tell them, 'The Kingdom of God is near you!'"* *(Luke 10:9 NIV)*

All that we've done by prayer and care gives us the credibility to share the love of Jesus; to let others know that we have a good, gracious, generous, life-giving King.

Desperados work the plan of Jesus, as He blesses with great joy and spiritual power.

THE DESPERADO DAILY

Ponder:

"So do not fear, for I am with you; do not be dismayed for I am your God. I will strengthen you and help you. I will uphold you with My righteous right hand. . .For I am the LORD, your God who takes hold of your right hand and says to you, 'Do not fear; I will help you." (Isaiah 41:10,13 NIV)

Practice:

Call down the goodness of God on those in your life who are far from the Lord. Build your relationships by building into people's lives. Meet their needs even if it takes a miracle. Share the love of Jesus.

Pray:

"Lord Jesus, thank you for the people You've placed in my life. I know You would love to reach them with Your saving love. Please use me. Show me ways to build into their lives, to meet their needs even if it requires Your miraculous power. I want them to know You as I know You. Help me to effectively share Your love. In Your name, Amen."

DESPERADO
DAY 27

No One is Beyond Help or Hope

LET'S JUST BE flat-out honest for a second. In a moment of dark desperation, have you ever said to yourself: "My life has not turned out the way I thought it would. It was not my plan to be an alcoholic when I started drinking in high school. It was not my plan to wreck my marriage when I got into pornography. It was not my plan to lose everything important in my life when I started doing drugs. On my wedding day, when I said my vows, divorce was not on my radar. When we had children, I never planned to be a single parent. Sadly, my life has not turned out the way I thought it would."

Do you ever ask, "How did I ever get so empty, worn-out and lost?"

Let me introduce you to three rodents that will wreck you, ruin you and run you ragged.

The first rodent is a rat. The surest way to live an empty life is to join the rat race. Even if you win, you're still a rat. Have you ever tried to climb the ladder of success? You do what you think you're supposed to do. You do what society says to do. You try to do it all the best you can. You go up rung after rung. I call them "rat" rungs. You grab hold and you climb up the rung of education. Nothing wrong with a good education. I would highly recommend it, but it will never fill that gaping hole in your heart. You just have a more educated empty. The next logical step is to grab hold and climb up the "rat" rung of a good job that pays good money. When you land that job, you find that there is still something missing. Maybe it's love. You grab hold of the "rat" rung of marriage and pull for all your worth. That doesn't fill your life like you thought it would. You're married and still empty. You grab hold and pull up on the rung of having children. But those little rats just become teenagers. You still feel empty. Sadly, the higher you go, the emptier you feel.

That's when you are tempted by the second rodent, the hamster. Have you ever seen a hamster on one of those wheels? This is how we do life worn-out. We try harder. We go faster. If our work doesn't satisfy, we double-down and work harder. Family leaves us unfulfilled, so we try harder at marriage, we try harder at parenting, we try harder and harder at providing and protecting. Now we're not just empty; we're exhausted.

Our response to inner emptiness and exhaustion can be to chase down rabbit trails of distraction and get lost. We play golf, go hunting and fishing, take up some hobby, play video games, follow our favorite sports team, over-shop, over-eat, over-anything. There is nothing wrong with golf (unless you play like me) or with any distracting activity. But you'll keep coming away empty if that's how you try to fill the gaping hole in your heart.

The gaping hole in your heart is shaped like a cross. We are all born with a cross-shaped hole in our hearts that can only be filled by the saving work of Jesus!

When our lives are empty shells, we must fill up on the words of Paul:

> "May you have the power to understand, as all God's people should, how wide, how long, how high and how deep His love is. May you experience the love of Christ, though it is too great to understand fully. Then you will be made complete with all the fullness of life and power that comes from God." (Ephesians 3:18,19 NLT)

When we are worn-out, we need to receive the rest and relaxation of Jesus. "Are you tired? Worn out? Burned out on religion? Come to Me. Get away with Me and you'll recover your life. I'll show you how to take a real rest. Walk with Me and work with Me — watch how I do it. Learn the unforced rhythms of grace. I won't lay anything heavy or ill-fitting on you. Keep company with Me and you'll learn to live freely and lightly." (Matthew 11:28-30 MSG)

When you feel lost, when you've climbed to the top of the ladder and you realize you're leaning against the wrong wall — the flimsiest of walls — look to Jesus, who promised: "For the Son of Man came to find and restore the lost!" (John 19:10 MSG)

The Son of Man is what Jesus most often called Himself. For, although He was fully God, Jesus was at the very same time fully human. Jesus is the God who came to be with us and was willing to become one of us.

Jesus came to find us no matter how far we have drifted from God. The word Jesus uses here for "restore" means "to rescue from harm and danger."

In fact, "lost" is a very strong word in Greek. The word Jesus uses is *"Apollumi"*, meaning *"a state of ruin or destruction."*

Jesus cannot stand the thought of you being lost and far from Him. Jesus desires all our friends and family to experience His abundant life. To Jesus, no one is beyond help or hope. Everyone is worth saving. Everyone has it in them to respond to His saving, rescuing love. Jesus wants to restore all of us to His best version of us.

Paul provides a compelling picture of our Jesus in His all-out effort to find us and rescue us from ruining our lives and eternities.

> *"Jesus...had equal status with God, but didn't think so much of Himself that He had to cling to the advantages of that status no matter what. Not at all. When the time came, He set aside the privileges of deity and took on the status of a slave, became human! Having become human, He stayed human. It was an incredibly humbling process. He didn't claim special privileges. Instead, He lived a selfless, obedient life and then died a selfless, obedient death — and the worst kind of death at that — a crucifixion. Because of that obedience, God lifted Him high and honored Him far above anyone or anything, ever, so that all created beings in heaven and on earth...will bow and worship before this Jesus Christ, and call out in praise that He is the Master of all, to the glorious honor of God the Father." (Phil. 2:6-11 MSG)*

Our relentless Jesus would let nothing stop Him from coming to save us. Though He is fully God, Jesus would become one of us, fully human. He would succeed completely in all the ways we have failed miserably. He would live a sinless life and save us from our empty rodent ways. He would fully fill the cross-shaped holes in our hearts with all the fullness of Himself and His saving love.

THE DESPERADO DAILY

Ponder:

> "May you have the power to understand, as all God's people should, how long, how wide, how high and how deep His love is. May you experience the love of Christ, though it is too great to understand fully. Then you will be made complete with all the fullness of life and power that comes from God." (Ephesians 3:18,19 NLT)

Practice:

Fill the cross-shaped hole in your heart with the fullness of Christ.

Pray:

> "Lord Jesus, I've spent too much of my life chasing my tail. Now I am in reckless pursuit of Your relentless love. My heart was made to be filled by You alone. Thank You for Your willingness to leave Your glory in heaven to become my Rescuer and restore my life. You are my Lord and King. I love You. In Your name I pray, Amen."

DESPERADO

DAY 28

A Search-and-Rescue Mission

JESUS IS ALWAYS on a relentless search-and-rescue mission. This is something I find irresistible about Him. I love it. Ever and again, when we find Jesus stalking through the pages of Luke, He is going the distance to save someone who wants to be saved. Nothing stops Jesus from creating His best version of the person in desperate need.

That is what's happening in today's Jesus story. This is a story of an exciting encounter between two desperados. One is Jesus, the Divine Desperado, driving Himself in the direction of a receptive human heart.

Jesus knows with absolute certainty that He and this other desperado are destined for a face-to-face meet. The other desperado can only pray in his wildest dreams to have a chance just to catch a glimpse of Jesus. Jesus is relentless. Nothing and no one can keep Him from getting to Zacchaeus, this other desperado who's desperate in his reckless pursuit of Jesus.

Zacchaeus' story is awesome news for us. As desperados, we recklessly pursue Jesus in worship. We recklessly pursue Him as we study His Word. We recklessly pursue Him as we serve others in His name. When we are in reckless pursuit of Jesus, He will let nothing stop Him from giving us a personal experience of Himself.

Luke gives us this record of the one-on-one between Zacchaeus and Jesus. *"Jesus entered Jericho and was passing THROUGH!"* (Luke 19:1 NIV)

Jesus might be passing through Jericho, but He'd never just pass by. I would never want to miss Jericho when we visit Israel. Jericho is like a green jewel in the middle of the desert. It has numerous natural springs in and around the city, making it a giant oasis. It is called the "City of Palms." Archeologists say it's the oldest continually inhabited city in the world.

Jesus entered Jericho and was passing through, because Jesus was making a bee-line to Jerusalem and to the cross waiting for Him there. Just before entering Jericho, Jesus made a staggering announcement to His closest followers. *"Jesus...took His twelve disciples aside and said to them, 'We are going up to Jerusalem and the Son of Man will be betrayed to the chief priests.... They will condemn Him to death and will turn Him over to the Romans to be mocked and flogged and crucified. On the third day, He will be raised to life!'"* (Matthew 20:17-19 NIV)

When Jesus said they'd go up to Jerusalem, He meant up. It was a hard, long, steep, 18 mile climb from Jericho to Jerusalem. Jericho is 850' below sea level. Jerusalem is 2500' above sea level. It was not the difficulty of the climb, the distance of the hike or the steep elevation gain that bothered Jesus. He was concerned about you. With each painstaking step, you were on His mind. He saw your face as He hiked. More importantly, He saw your sin. He saw you destined for hell. He went up for you.

Jesus saw your desperate need for a Savior. He was going through Jericho to Jerusalem to die on a cross to pay for all your sin. Three days later God would raise Him from the dead. But make no mistake. It was all for you.

In our story, something very interesting happens in Jericho, compelling Jesus to stay overnight. We learn what moves Jesus to set aside His personal agenda. He puts everything on hold; he adjusts His schedule to seek and save one lost sinner from hell. *"A man was there by the name of Zacchaeus; he was a chief tax collector and was wealthy!"* (Luke 19:2 NIV)

When it says Zacchaeus is wealthy, it means filthy rich. I'm guessing he is the richest man in Jericho and one of the richest men in the entire country. He is also one of the most hated men in the entire country. He's a chief tax collector. He could not get any higher on the rich and powerful scale. He could not get any lower as a social outcast.

In that day tax collectors were deemed the worst kind of traitors — Jewish men who had gone to work for the Roman government. With one hand, they taxed you for Rome. With the other hand, they levied any tax they could think of for themselves. They taxed everything you possessed — the number of animals pulling your cart to market, the number of wheels on your cart, the axle that held the wheels, the cart itself and everything in it.

Tax collectors made a good living, squeezing money out of their own people. But Zacchaeus was a chief tax collector. That's why he was off-the-charts rich. There were three major tax regions in Israel. He was the top dog in the Jericho region, getting a cut of every tax collector's take in his entire region. He was so hated he was not allowed to attend worship. He was seen as more unclean than a leper, considered defiled, an outcast. No one would socialize with him but other tax collectors.

But he had heard of this Jesus — a miracle-worker, mighty in word and deed, God's man on earth. Rumor had it that Jesus was a friend of tax collectors, but Jesus did not care what anyone said. He would enter a tax collector's house without a second thought. Word on the street was that Jesus even partied with tax collectors. Zacchaeus had to see this Jesus.

"He wanted to see who Jesus was, but being a short man he could not because of the crowd. So he ran ahead and climbed a sycamore-fig tree to see Him, since Jesus was coming that way." (Luke 19:3,4 NIV)

This is not just a story from ages past. This is your story. Jesus is coming your way. He is seeking you out. He longs to lead you into His dream for your life. He has plans to rescue you from whatever destructive ruin you have experienced. Jesus is more than ready to make an amazing appearance in your life right where you need Him most. He simply waits for you to get desperate to see Him.

"'When you come looking for Me, you will find Me. When you get serious about finding Me and want it more than anything else, I will make sure you are not disappointed. I will turn things around for you!'" (Jeremiah 29:13,14 MSG)

THE DESPERADO DAILY

Ponder:

> "When you come looking for Me, you will find Me. When you get serious about finding Me and want it more than anything else, I'll make sure you're not disappointed. I will turn things around for you!" (Jeremiah 29:13.14 MSG)

Practice:

Get serious about finding Jesus and want it more than anything else.

Pray:

> "Dear Jesus, I believe You are a turn-around specialist. You can turn around any area of my life where I seek you with all my heart. Thank You for all You've done and continue to do to save me and lead me into Your dream for my life. In Your name, Amen."

[168] *Desperado*

DESPERADO

DAY 29

We Stand,
the Lord Fights,
We Win

THE STAGE IS set. Two desperados have a divinely designed date with each other. One, Zacchaeus, is up a tree,
desperate to see a Savior. The other, Jesus, on His way, is
desperate to save. The man up the tree is like a magnet,
drawing Jesus to himself. He placed himself in an advan-
tageous position to see Jesus. The same is true of you.
As you read this book right now, you are well-positioned
for a deeply personal face-to-face with Jesus. Jesus has
been dreaming of having this moment with you for all
your life.

I want you to feel yourself in the story and out on a
limb with Zacchaeus. What happens to this tax collector in a very real way can happen to you. Three things
happen.

"Jesus reached the spot..." (Luke 19:5 NIV). Something
life-changing was about to happen as Jesus reached the

spot where Zacchaeus had prepared to see Him. Being prepared for an encounter with Jesus is everything. Take a moment and spiritually place yourself at the spot where you can have a heart-to-heart with the Lord of life.

"*(Jesus) looked up...*" (Luke 19:5) The Lord knew right where to find Zacchaeus, just like He knows right where to find you. Jesus is drawn to you by your desperation.

"*(Jesus) said to him, 'Zacchaeus...*" (Luke 19:5 NIV). They had never met, yet Jesus knows Zacchaeus by name and calls him by name. What do you think it did to Zack to have Jesus — in front of everyone — call him by name? What does it do to you to know that Jesus is whispering your name over your soul right this moment?

"*'Zacchaeus, come down immediately. I must stay at your house today!'*" (Luke 19:5 NIV)

When Jesus said, "I must," He used a word that meant, "It is an absolute necessity that I stay at your house today." This is your moment, Zacchaeus. Don't miss this moment. If you seize this moment with Me, I will change your life forever from the inside-out.

God has arranged for you to be reading this book today. God has called you into this reckless pursuit of His Son. What Jesus said to Zacchaeus He's saying to you right now. "This is your moment with Me. Don't miss it. Seize this moment with Me and I will change your life forever from the inside-out."

Zacchaeus didn't have to think twice. "*He came down at once and welcomed Jesus gladly.*" (Luke 19:6 NIV) No one saw this coming in their wildest dreams — not the crowd on the street or the crowd following Jesus. They all were totally stunned when Jesus publicly announced that He was staying at the house of Zacchaeus. The word Jesus used meant He was staying for the night. Only dear friends would invite themselves over to someone's house for the night. This is huge, because *"A friend loves at all times!"* (Prov. 17:17)

This is a prelude to how Jesus would prove His unfailing love for Zacchaeus and for us. *"There is no greater love than to lay down one's life for one's friends."* (John 15:13)

Zacchaeus is a social outcast. He is deemed defiled. If you go to his house, then you are defiled as well by mere association. Jesus is saying, "Zacchaeus, I want to be your new best friend and I don't care who knows it. I don't care what it costs Me." But this is just like Jesus. It's why He is called the Friend that sticks closer than a brother. Jesus is offering you His friendship as well. Zacchaeus accepted the offer, which did not go over so well with the crowds.

"All the people saw this and began to mutter, 'He has gone to be the guest of a sinner." (Luke 19:7 NIV)

We don't know what happens next. We don't know what Jesus said to Zacchaeus behind closed doors, but I think I can make a pretty good guess. Maybe as they sat down over a delicious dinner, Jesus said, "Zacchaeus, My friend, I have come to BRING you the saving love of God. You're not a social outcast to God. You BELONG! In fact, I want you to change the direction of your empty, lost life and SERVE Me by serving others. I want our friendship to GROW!"

Whatever Jesus said, this is how Zacchaeus responded. *"Zacchaeus stood up and said to the Lord, 'Look, Lord. Here and now I give half of my possessions to the poor..."* (Luke 19:8 NIV)

This was irrefutable evidence that Zack was now a desperado. It's evidence we offer every weekend at the church I serve. We give a few extra dollars of generosity to help people in desperate need in our community. Every three months we do a big love offering to make a significant impact — here and now — for hurting children, for hungry people and for people far from God. We want to bless what the Lord wants blessed.

We want to hear for us what Jesus said to Zacchaeus. *"Jesus said to him, 'Today salvation has come to this house.... For the Son of Man came to seek and to save what was lost.'"* (Luke 19:9,10 NIV)

Did you know historians say that Zacchaeus later became the pastor of the church in Caesarea by the sea? I don't know if you caught the phrase earlier. Let me show it to you again. *"Zacchaeus stood up..."* The force of the Greek verb used here means that Zacchaeus took a stand for Jesus and got very generous with those in need.

That's what desperados are all about — taking a stand for Jesus. Over and over the Word of God declares the benefits of taking a stand for the Lord. *"Do not be afraid. STAND firm and you will see the deliverance the LORD will bring you today...The LORD will fight for you; you need only to (STAND) still."* (Exodus 14:13,14 NIV)

Again, in II Chronicles 20:17 we find the desperado battle plan. We stand. The LORD fights. We win. "You will not have to fight this battle. Take up your positions; STAND firm and see the deliverance the LORD will give you!" Jesus likely said to Zacchaeus what He promises all desperados: "He who STANDS firm to the end will be saved!" (Matthew 10:22 NIV) So we stand. The Lord fights. We win.

THE DESPERADO DAILY

Ponder:

"He who stands firm to the end will be saved!" (Matthew 10:22 NIV)

Practice:

Stand up for Jesus and see the deliverance the Lord will give you!

Pray:

"Dear Jesus, thank You for loving me like a dear friend, loving me all the time no matter what. Thank You for being my Friend that stays closer than a brother. Mostly, Lord, I thank You for showing me the greatest extent of friendship, laying down Your life for my sins. I love You. I recklessly pursue Your relentless love. In Your name, Amen."

DESPERADO
DAY 30

A "What if" Adventure

I HAVE A huge question. When it comes to us leaning into our future fully, freely and filled with hope, this is the quintessential question. The question is this: What if?

Before I lead you off on a "what if" adventure, I have another important question to ask: What is it that most holds you back or holds you down in life?

How would you answer that question, if you cannot blame others and you cannot make excuses? These are two of the big barriers to moving forward in life. Blaming others for your life holds you back. Making excuses holds you down. If you could be completely honest and it's just on you, what most holds you back and holds you down in life? Is it fear and worry holding you back? Is it anxiety and anger holding you down? Is it loads of pain and a lack of peace holding you back? Is it great guilt or unshakable shame holding you down? What is it that most holds you back or holds you down in life?

Now let's play "What if?" What if there was a place you could go every week where you would find peace from the fear and worry, where you could get a spiritual power to overcome the anxiety and anger? What if there was a place like that? What if, in that place, there was a person who would heal you from the inside-out and help you overcome your past and give you hope for your future? What if, in that place of peace with that powerful, healing, helpful person, there was something you could personally practice to be fully forgiven and completely cleansed of all guilt and shame? If there was such a place of peace, would you go each week and meet with that One who heals and helps? Would you do whatever it takes to find full forgiveness and freedom from all guilt and shame?

To tell you the truth, we don't have to play the "what if" game. There is a place you can go, a Person you can meet with every week and a practice you can do to get free of all that holds you back and holds you down in life.

I want to tell you a Jesus story to explain how this works. But before I tell you the Jesus story, I must tell you the backstory — the way, way, way backstory — the story of Jesus, God the Father and the Holy Spirit before time began — before the cosmos was created, before there was a planet earth or a humanity to fill it.

To hear this story, you must join me in my inspired imagination. I imagine before one hint of history happens, there is a huge heavenly arena, filled to capacity with tens of thousands of angels, all on their feet, joyously, powerfully proclaiming praises to God the Father; Jesus, God the Son; and God the Holy Spirit. Fully surrounded by all the angels of heaven at center stage are the Father,

Son and Spirit, holding hands together; all three are prancing and dancing with great rejoicing.

Even above the wild worship of the angels, we can hear God singing, "I give You glory, Holy Spirit." The Holy Spirit sings, "I give You glory, Lord Jesus." Jesus sings, "I give You glory, Heavenly Father." God the Father sings back, "I love You, Jesus." Jesus sings, "I love You, Holy Spirit." The Holy Spirit sings, "I love You, Heavenly Father."

All this God-dancing becomes a divine dervish, when suddenly all three persons of the Godhead shout out together, "We want to love even more! With open hearts, we open our arms." Together they breathed these words, *"Let us make human beings in our image, make them reflecting our nature!"* (Genesis 1:26 MSG) "Let us love more."

No sooner are those words spoken than the dance is done. Father, Son and Spirit fall to Their knees and bow Their heads together. Simultaneously, they begin to convulse and shudder and say, "Their rejection of us will be like spitting in our face. They will sin and die. Their rebellion against us will be a sick, sinister slap in the face. We need a plan to save them from their sin." The Holy Spirit weeps, but lifts His head and says, "With loving kindness I will make them aware of their sin and their need for God." Jesus weeps as well. Lifting His head, He whispers, "I will become one of them. I will live a perfect life for them and then give My life in death as full payment for their sin. I will be their substitute. I will take the death they deserve." Through His tears God the Father lifts His head and declares, "I will raise You from the dead. I will give You the Name above all names and exalt You to the highest place. I will forgive their sins and cleanse them of all shame. Those who surrender to

You, Jesus, will be My children and I will be their Father in heaven. I will fill them with our Holy Spirit. As they give their lives to Me, I'll never stop giving life to them."

That's how I fantasize what happened, but here's what we know as facts. Here are a few snippets from a prayer Jesus prayed the night before He was executed.

"Father, glorify Me with Your very own splendor, the very splendor I had in Your presence BEFORE there was a world." (John 17:5 MSG)

"Father...You loved Me BEFORE the creation of the world!" (John 17:24 NIV)

Here's how the Apostle Paul throws light on this way, way, way backstory: *"Long BEFORE He laid down the earth's foundation, God had us in mind, had settled on us as the focus of His love...He wanted us to enter into the celebration of His lavish gift-giving by the hand of His beloved Son."* (Ephesians 1:4,6 MSG)

Before the world began, as the Three-in-One God danced, the Father and Son dropped hands to invite us into their circle of love. Jesus willingly died to make it all possible. That's why the book of Revelation introduces Jesus as *"The Lamb who was slain from the creation of the world."* (Revelation 13:8 NIV)

Here's the good news. This is not about a big "what if". This is the ultimate "what is." *"Christ is the visible expression of the invisible God. He existed before creation began....It is in Christ that the full nature of God chose to live, and through Him God planned to reconcile in His own person...everything on earth and everything in heaven by virtue of the sacrifice of the cross."* (Colossians 1:15, 17, 19, 20 J.B. Phillips)

THE DESPERADO DAILY

Ponder:

"Christ is the visible expression of the invisible God. He existed before creation began.... It is in Christ that the full nature of God chose to live, and through Him God planned to reconcile in His own person...everything on earth and everything in heaven by virtue of the sacrifice of the cross." (Colossians 1:15,17,19,20 J.B. Phillips)

Practice:

Refuse to make excuses or blame others for the condition of your life. Choose to accept the incredible invitation of Jesus to enter a life-giving relationship with God the Father and be filled with the Holy Spirit, giving glory and praise to the Three-in-One.

Pray:

"Lord Jesus, what a thought — that You would think of me before the world began; that You would want me with all Your heart, even knowing what a vile sinner I would be; that You would be willing to die for me to pay for my sins and bring me into relationship with God; that I could be cleansed of shame and be filled with the Holy Spirit. You are love itself. I love You. I pursue You with reckless abandon. In Your name, Amen."

DESPERADO
DAY 31

Marked by
the Blood

YESTERDAY WE DID the way, way, way backstory that sets up our Jesus story. This Jesus story is a dinner story. Jesus is hosting a holiday dinner. The main course is lamb.

Have you ever prepared a lamb dinner? There are likely two big differences between your lamb dinner and this lamb dinner hosted by Jesus. First, Jesus is the Lamb of God, who would be slain for the sins of the world. His lamb dinner carried great significance. It points to His sacrificial death to save us from eternal death.

Secondly, I bet you had leftovers from your lamb dinner. In the lamb dinner hosted by Jesus there could be no leftovers. Every bite of lamb had to be consumed by those at the meal. It was a foreshadowing of Jesus' death being more than physical death. He would be completely consumed by all God's anger due us, all God's judgment due us, all God's condemnation due us for our sin, when He died in our place on the cross.

In addition, in this meal none of the lamb's bones could be broken. Why? The lamb served as a picture of Jesus of whom it was prophesied, *"He keeps all His bones. Not one of them was broken."* (Psalm 34:20 ESV)

Remember when Jesus was executed, the thieves on either side of Him had their legs broken to expedite their deaths. But when they went to break the legs of Jesus, He was already dead. He kept all His bones. Not one of them was broken.

Maybe you ask, "Why lamb? Why not T-bone steak or a shrimp kabob or sushi?" There is another backstory. Not a way, way, way backstory; but this is back 1,500 years. Isn't that wild? Every year for 1,500 years the Jewish people had celebrated this special day called Passover. The lamb served at the dinner was the Passover lamb.

Let me nutshell the backstory for you. 1,500 years earlier, the Jewish people had been bound in slavery down in Egypt, but God miraculously intervened in their behalf. He used His man, Moses. Moses went head to head with the king of Egypt. Moses said, "You better set God's people free or bad stuff will happen to you." The king of Egypt said, "Take your best shot, dude. I'm calling your bluff." This happened nine times and every time something horribly bad happened to the Egyptians, when the king refused to free God's people.

Then came the tenth time. This was the mother of all bad stuff. The angel of death was coming to kill the firstborn son in every family. The firstborn son pointed to Jesus — the one and only Son of God.

But here was the good deal for God's people. Their families would be spared if they took a lamb, split open its belly and wiped the blood of the lamb on the doors of their homes. God's people were to roast the lamb and eat every last bite for dinner.

This all went down just like God said it would. A death angel came. Firstborn sons died. Except the death angel "passed over" every home marked by the blood of the lamb. In those homes every firstborn son lived.

This points to the saving, shed blood of Jesus on the cross. When we have it applied to our lives, death passes over us and God grants us life forever.

The purpose of the Passover was to remember how God saved His people from death through the death of an innocent substitute. That's the significance of the Passover meal and the Passover lamb. It is also the exact point of the regular experience of the Lord's Supper. We remember the crucifixion of Jesus. He took our place as our innocent substitute on the cross, getting the death we deserved for our sin.

All this gets us ready for our Jesus dinner story. *"When the hour came, Jesus and His apostles reclined at the table."* (Luke 22:14 NIV)

The hour Passover began was at sunset with daylight fading and darkness creeping in. Jesus and all His men lean on their elbows as they recline on cushions with their feet away from the table for obvious reasons. As host, Jesus is at the head of the table.

Here are the first words from His lips, *"I have eagerly desired to eat this Passover with you before I suffer. For I tell you, I will not eat it again until it finds fulfillment in the Kingdom of God."* (Luke 22:15,16 NIV)

Something's going on here. These are not the traditional first words of the Passover experience. Even though Jesus is anything but traditional, there is so much emotion in His voice that His men are more than a bit shaken by His announcement.

Jesus is using very passionate language. The phrase, "I have eagerly desired," is very strong in the Greek. It might be better translated, "With desire, I have desired."

Jesus knows that in less than 24 hours He will be dangling and dying on a criminal's cross. This is His last chance to do something of eternal impact with His close friends.

When He says, "I will not eat it again," He uses the strongest possible Greek negative. In other words, "Never, never, never will I eat this meal again."

Something big is happening here. What's going on? Jesus is intensely passionate about this moment in the making. He is putting an absolute end to a 1,500-year-old tradition and way of life. At the very same time He is establishing something completely new, deeply personal and relational, and spiritually profound, which will have an eternal impact for all generations of Christ-followers to come.

What Jesus is about to do here has tremendous implications for us. It shows us how to wring every drop of meaning and blessing out of the Lord's Supper as we experience it each weekend. It's why the Apostle Paul counsels us: *"Examine your motives, test your heart, come to this meal in holy awe!"* (I Corinthians 11:28 MSG)

THE DESPERADO DAILY

Ponder:

> *"Examine your motives, test your heart, come to this meal in holy awe!"* (I Corinthians 11:28 MSG)

Practice:

Always take advantage of every opportunity to participate in the Lord's Supper.

There is saving power in rightly remembering the crucifixion of Jesus, celebrating the forgiveness of Jesus, and regularly re-committing to recklessly pursue the love of Jesus.

Pray:

> *"Dear Jesus, there is no one and nothing compared to You. Only You could take a bit of bread and a sip of grape juice and make it amazingly meaningful. You broke the bread to symbolize the brutality You suffered in behalf of my sin. You blessed the wine to represent Your blood shed to erase any evidence of my sin. Thank You both for Your sacrifice on the cross and a way to regularly remember it. In Your Name, Amen."*

DESPERADO

DAY 32

A Meal We Won't Want to Miss

I LOVE TO eat. I'm addicted to food. I only have so many meals left in my life and I don't want to miss even one. My favorite meals have little to do with what is served and everything to do with who is joining me. The best meals are with those I love best.

That's why the Lord's supper is one of my favorite meals every week in worship. I get to do it with my favorite fellow desperados. People I'm with make the experience precious. But practicing the process Jesus put in place gives this spiritual meal special power.

The first thing Jesus does is what any host would do at a Passover meal. Jesus offers a prayer of thanks to God. This is the best way for us to prepare for our experience of the Lord's Supper each weekend: Offer a prayer of thanksgiving!

Thank God for His goodness and grace; thank God for His presence, His protection, provision and the peace that passes all understanding. Thank God for His mercy, His forgiveness, His unfailing love and everything else that comes to mind.

The second thing Jesus would do is offer what we might call a toast. He would lift a cup of wine. This was called the cup of blessing. It was the first of four cups for the meal. The wine was doubly diluted with water — a part wine, two parts water — more like our grape juice. This was not a meal for drunkenness. This was a meal to mindfully celebrate the blessings of God!

This is an excellent next step for us as we prepare to take the Lord's Supper in worship. We don't merely thank God. We begin to worship God for how He blesses us with all that money cannot buy — love, joy, goodness, hope, strength, wisdom and kindness.

Then at this meal Jesus would initiate the ritual of the washing of hands. Each person around the table would wash their hands as a symbol of their need for inner cleansing from guilt and shame, the need of forgiveness for any wrong word, deed or thought.

This is a good place for us to go spiritually as we prepare to take the Lord's Supper each week: Admit our need to be cleansed by God of our guilt and shame.

Then Jesus does something in the meal that had never been done before. It must have staggered His friends to the core of their very being. Here's how Luke explains it. *"He took bread, gave thanks and broke it, and gave it to them saying, 'This is My body given for you; do this in remembrance of Me.'"* (Luke 22:19 NIV) Something old was absolutely over. All of history had changed in this moment. Jesus established something all new, creating this act of remembrance — eating a bit of bread to focus all thought on how He'd die in our place, as our substitute, to pay for our sin.

Then Jesus led them in the rest of the meal. They would sing songs from Scripture and drink a second cup of wine. Jesus would have told the story of what all this meant and why God's people did it. They would then eat the lamb with the bread dipped in a bitter herb, something like our horseradish. There would be a third cup of wine and more singing. Then Jesus laid down the second mind-blower of the meal, as Luke records it.

"After the supper, He took the cup, saying, 'This is a new covenant in My blood, which is poured out for you!'" (Luke 22:20 NIV)

That's it from Luke. Matthew, Mark and John also describe the Lord's Supper. But Luke gives us the most microwaved version of this memorial meal. There's a reason for this. Luke's best friend, the Apostle Paul, ten years earlier had written of communion in exact detail. Let me share with you the first full accounting of the Lord's Supper.

> *"For I received from the Lord what I also passed on to you. The Lord Jesus, on the night He was betrayed, took bread, and when He had given thanks, He broke it and said, 'This is My body, which is for you; do this in remembrance of Me.' In the same way, after the supper He took the cup, saying: 'This cup is the new covenant in My blood; do this, whenever you drink it, in remembrance of Me. For whenever you eat this bread and drink this cup, you proclaim the Lord's death until He comes!'"* (I Corinthians 11:23-26 NIV)

Let's pay close attention to each element Paul emphasizes for what communion means.

The purpose of the Lord's Supper is to ponder and participate in the Lord's death! As we ponder the work of the Lord's death in our behalf, our hearts swell with gratitude. Paul put it this way: *"Is not the cup of thanksgiving for which we give thanks a participation in the blood of Christ? And is not the bread that we break a participation in the body of Christ?"* (I Corinthians 10:16 NIV)

The Lord's Supper is a hands-on practice of proclaiming the Lord's death! Whenever we share in the bread and cup of communion, it is a new enunciation of the good news of Jesus, which *"is the power of God for the salvation of everyone who believes."* (Romans 1:16 NIV)

In our regular observance of communion, we experience God's peace and power. Are you stressed, worried, or afraid? This is your on-going source of God's peace. Are you hurting and broken? Share in the Lord's Supper and share in His healing power.

"He was pierced for our transgressions; He was crushed for our iniquities; the punishment that brought us peace was upon Him and by His wounds we are healed!" (Isaiah 53:5 NIV)

All of us, more times than we can count, have sinned against our holy God. But with that bite of bread, we receive a fresh flow of full forgiveness. With that sip of juice, we are cleansed of all guilt and shame. *"Every one of us have strayed away...left God's path to follow our own. Yet God laid on Him the guilt and sins of every one of us!"* (Isaiah 53:6 LB)

THE DESPERADO DAILY

Ponder:

> *"He was pierced for our transgressions; He was crushed for our iniquities; the punishment that brought us peace was upon Him and by His wounds we are healed. Every one of us have strayed away...left God's path to follow our own. Yet God laid on Him the guilt and sins of every one of us!"* (Isaiah 53:5,6 NIV)

Practice:

Commune with your Lord regularly. Let your heart swell with thanks as you ponder the death of Jesus, trying to feel what He felt, as He suffered for you. Never neglect an opportunity to personally proclaim the saving power of the Lord's death.

Pray:

> *"Lord Jesus, Cosmos-Creator, Cross-Bearer, Suffering Savior, Victorious Risen Lord. Your lavish love has no limits. I praise You for making a memorial meal, so I can freely express my thanks for Your sacrificial work. In communion with You, I always get more than I give — more peace, more healing, more hope and joy. In Your Name, Amen."*

DESPERADO
DAY 33

Set Yourself Up

HERE'S WHAT I believe: God is up to something big in your life!

I believe this to be true because the Sovereign Lord has you reading this book. This is no accident. He has kept you reading, learning, growing as a desperado for Jesus. This is no coincidence. This is no fluke. This is God up to something big in your life.

God Himself lays out this exciting reality in detail. *"'I know the plans I have for you,' declares the LORD, 'plans to prosper you and not to harm you, plans to give you hope and a future!'"* (Jeremiah 29:11 NIV)

This tells me God has planned for you to be on this adventurous journey with Jesus. God is up to something big in your life. He has plans to prosper you relentlessly, to protect you relentlessly, to give you hope and a future, even though life goes wrong.

You ask, "Okay, say I believe God is up to something big in my life. How big?" Big enough to blow your mind. God is up to something bigger than you ever dreamed. *"(God) is able to do immeasurably more than all we ask or*

imagine, according to His power that is at work within us!"
(Ephesians 3:20 NIV)

Maybe you say, "God is able. That means God can.
But will God? God can, but will He?" To tell you the
truth, that part is strictly up to you. Listen to this promise. *"All that happens to us is working to our good, if we
love God and are fitting into His plans."* (Romans 8:28 LB)

God longs to work everything together for good in
your life, if you will let Him.

Maybe you have one final question. Maybe you want
to know: "Why would God even think of doing something big in someone like me? Why would God give my
lousy life a second thought? I'm not exactly what you
would call God material."

I have the best kind of news for you: *"God demon-
strates His own love for us in this: While we were still sinners, Christ died for us!"* (Romans 5:8 NIV)

God does not wait for us to be good enough before He
does something big in our lives!

In fact, I want to explain how you can set God free to
do something immeasurably big in your life. I'll do that
by taking you into four separate scenes from the day Jesus died.

As the curtain is pulled back on the first scene, we see
two kings. One is an earthly king; one is heaven's King of
kings. The earthly king is called Herod. He has limited
power; heaven's King of kings is Jesus. He has unlimited
authority. King Herod is surrounded by servants. King
Jesus is surrounded by soldiers. King Herod won't shut-
up. King Jesus won't say a word. On this morning King
Herod has already had breakfast. King Jesus has already
been beaten bloody.

Do you know what Jesus would love to say to Herod, if the little, limited earthly king would listen? Jesus would love to say: "'I know the plans I have for you, Herod, plans to prosper you and not to harm you, plans to give you hope and a future.'"

I believe the real reason Jesus stood before Herod was to save Herod from sin, from death and hell. This is Herod's opportunity to bow before Jesus as Lord and Savior. But Herod won't worship Jesus; he only wants to use Jesus for his own pleasure.

"When King Herod saw Jesus, he was greatly pleased, because for a long time he had been wanting to see Him. From what he had heard about Jesus, he hoped to see Him perform some miracle. He plied Jesus with many questions, but JESUS GAVE HIM NO ANSWER." (Luke 23:8,9 NIV)

When you only want Jesus for what you can get, you get nothing. Being all about yourself can stop God from doing something big in your life!

There's more to this scene. *"The high priests and religious scholars were right there, saying their piece, strident and shrill in their accusations."* (Luke 23:10)

The religious, holier-than-thous have entered the spiritual danger zone with Herod. Attacking Jesus keeps God from doing something big in your life!

It is so huge that you are reading this book about following Jesus. Your willingness to learn and grow is proof that you are not attacking Jesus. You are attracted to Jesus. You have, thus, set yourself up to free God to do something big in your life.

In this first scene there are also soldiers. *"Mightily offended, Herod turned on Jesus. His soldiers joined in, taunting and jeering."* (Luke 23:11 MSG)

These soldiers are up in Jesus' face. Do you know what they're saying to Him, when they taunt Him and jeer Him? They're saying, "Jesus, You're nobody. You're from nowhere. You've got nothing. Jesus, You are nothing."

How do I know that's what they said? There is a Greek word in the text. It has a root word. The root word is "ekouden," meaning "from nothing."

This is where we began in our understanding of what it means to follow Jesus. In the day of Jesus an "ekouden" was someone who had nothing but was desperate enough to would take reckless action to get something of substance for their lives.

That was our Jesus, the divine Desperado, desperate for our salvation. That's us. We are committed to being desperados, recklessly pursuing our relentless Jesus. The good news is: When life's a battle, we're on the winning side. Final victory is ours with Jesus.

THE DESPERADO DAILY

Ponder:

"I'll show up and take care of you, as I promised, and bring you back home. I know what I'm doing. I have it all planned out — plans to take care of you, not abandon you, plans to give you the future you hope for." (Jeremiah 29:10,11 MSG)

Practice:

Claim the promise of what God says next in Jeremiah 29. "When you call on Me, when you come and pray to Me, I'll listen. When you come looking for Me, you'll find Me. Yes, when you get serious about finding Me and want it more than anything else, I'll make sure you won't be disappointed." (Jeremiah 29:12,13 MSG)

Pray:

"Dear Jesus, I pursue You with all my heart, because I want to be more like You.

When I watch You on the day of Your death, You stand unimpressed before a king full of self-importance. You stand with soldiers, unintimidated by their mocking threats. You stand unafraid in the face of religious accusations. Be my confidence, peace and hope. I want to stand up for You and with You. Help me stand. In Your name, Amen."

DESPERADO

DAY 34

Lavished Love

THROUGHOUT THIS BOOK, I wanted one truth to stand out: Jesus is the Divine Desperado!

His relentless love for us compelled Him to leave heaven and become nothing, human, one of us. In His undying desperation to save us from our sinful self-destruction, He recklessly laid down His life on a criminal's cross, sacrificing Himself in our place, as our substitute. We deserve to suffer agonizing, hellish consequences for our sin. But Jesus willingly took upon Himself all the punishment due us. How can we not simply love this incredible Christ with heartfelt devotion? We choose to be desperados for Jesus because He first became a desperado for us.

This is the major mistake Herod makes as the curtain closes on the first scene in the day our Lord was crucified. In truth, Jesus was dying to be Herod's Savior. King Jesus gives King Herod a chance, like He lovingly gives us all a chance. Herod blows off the King of kings, laughs in His face; he doesn't allow Jesus to do anything in his life. This is our lesson: We must choose for Jesus to do something big in our lives.

Scene two is a shouting match. Scene two is a governor and a grunt. Pilate is the governor. Jesus is the grunt — a nobody with nothing but a desperate desire to die for the sins of the world. In this scene, no one cares about what Jesus cares about.

> "Pilate called in the high priests, rulers and others and said, 'You brought this Man to me as a disturber of the peace. I examined Him in front of all of you and found there was nothing to your charge.... It's clear He's done nothing wrong, let alone anything deserving death. I'm going to warn Him...and let Him go. At that the crowd went wild: 'Kill Him!'.... Pilate still wanted to let Jesus go, and so spoke out again. But they kept shouting back, 'Crucify Him! Crucify Him!' Pilate tried a third time, 'But for what crime? I've found nothing in Him deserving death. I'm going to warn Him...and let Him go.' But they kept at it, a shouting mob, demanding that He be crucified. Finally, they shouted Pilate down. He CAVED IN and gave them what they wanted." (Luke 23:13-25 MSG)

Here's a big question. Do you think Jesus would love to do something big in the lives of these angry religious fanatics who want Him dead? Absolutely. But they are so full of anger, there's no room in them for Jesus to do anything.

Pilate caves in. In all the rubble and debris of his collapsed character, there's no room for Jesus to do anything.

Something spiritually profound is going on just beneath the surface in scene two. The native language of the angry religious fanatics is Hebrew. The Hebrew word for heaven is "Shamayim". Here is the important insight. When a Hebrew word ends in "im", it is plural, like an English word ending with the letter "s". The point is: the things of heaven are above, above, above, unending, unending, unending, unlimited, unlimited, unlimited.

On the other hand, the Hebrew word for earth is "aretz." "Aretz" is not plural. It is singular — one earth. Earth has boundaries. The things of earth are narrowly limited.

The religious fanatics are full of anger, because their hearts are set on the things of earth. Pilate caves in to their anger because his mind is focused on the things of earth.

The same can be true of us. We can handcuff Jesus from doing anything in our lives to the degree we focus on the narrow boundaries and temporary realities of this world.

Here's the exciting, good news. Jesus is free to do something big in our lives, as we focus our lives on the unbounded things of heaven.

The same Apostle who wrote these words about the Lord, *"who is able to do immeasurably more than all we ask or imagine…"* (Ephesians 3:20 NIV) also wrote: *"If you believe in goodness and if you value the approval of God, fix your minds on the things which are holy and right and pure and beautiful and good. Model your conduct on what you have learned…and you will find the God of peace will be with you!"* (Philippians 4:8 J.B. Phillips NT)

What happens next in this second scene is of supreme significance. It is so important it is told and retold in all four accounts of Jesus' death. I don't identify with Pilate. You do not identify with the religious freaks. But at this point in the story, we find ourselves personally a part in the plot.

Matthew sets up the dramatic moment. *"It was the governor's custom at the Feast to release a prisoner chosen by the crowd. At the time they had a notorious prisoner, called Barabbas. When the crowd had gathered, Pilate asked them, 'Which one do you want me to release to you: Barabbas, or Jesus?'...'Barabbas,' they answered. 'What shall I do, then, with Jesus...?' Pilate asked. They all answered, 'Crucify Him!' Then he released Barabbas to them. But he had Jesus flogged and handed Him over to be crucified."* (Matt. 27:15-17; 21,22,26 NIV)

Why would God Almighty breathe this specific part of the story into the heart of each gospel-writer — Matthew, Mark, Luke and John? This is our part of the story, which the Lord wants no one to miss. Barabbas is us and we are Barabbas. Think about it. Barabbas is a rebel. We have rebelled against God. Barabbas is a notorious criminal. We are notorious sinners. Barabbas is the guilty one. We are the guilty. Barabbas was condemned to die. Our sin has condemned us to death. Barabbas deserved to die. We deserve eternal death. Barabbas is given his freedom, when the only innocent One takes his place. On the cross, Jesus takes our place, offering us freedom from death and hell. Barabbas gets mercy. He is protected from the consequences of all he's done wrong. When we trust in the work of Christ on the cross, we get merciful protection from the punishment we deserve for our sin. Barabbas gets grace. His freedom is a gift he does not deserve. When we surrender to Jesus, we are graced with all that we don't deserve — an abundance of His relentless love, joy, peace, goodness, hope. The name, Barabbas, means "son of the father." *"How great is the love the Father has lavished on us, that we should be called children of God! And that is what we are!"* (I John 3:1 NIV)

THE DESPERADO DAILY

Ponder:

"How great is the love the Father has lavished on us, that we should be called children of God. And that is what we are!" (I John 3:1 NIV)

Practice:

Choose for Jesus to do something big in your life.

Pray:

"Dear Jesus, religion always wants to kill You. The government never knows what to do with You. You are the only utterly innocent One. You knew no sin. You did no sin. Yet You willingly took our place to pay for our sin. We get free, we get mercy and grace, we get cleansed and forgiven, we get eternal life. Like Barabbas, we shake our heads in wonder. We never saw this coming. We'll always love You. In Your name, Amen."

DESPERADO

DAY 35

Will You Touch the Cross of Christ?

IF THE THIRD scene in the drama of the death of Christ had a soundtrack, it might be this old hymn: "Must Jesus bear the cross alone, and all the world go free? No, there's a cross for everyone, and there's a cross for me. The consecrated cross I'll bear till death shall set me free; and then go home my crown to wear, for there's a crown for me."

Desperados bear a temporary cross for Christ and receive an eternal crown from Christ!

If scene three had a flashback, we'd find it at the Gates of Hell. That's the place where Jesus had led His followers one year earlier. It was just on the outskirts of Caesarea Philippi. People came there from far and wide to worship pagan gods, believing the gods of the underworld entered their world through a dark cave, called the Gates of Hell. If you go there today, you can still find the ruins of the idols worshipped there.

People were convinced that if they prayed hard enough, danced fast enough, screamed loud enough, the gods of the underworld would come up to bless them, protect them and make them prosper. It was a devil of a place. But it was at this very place that three firsts occurred.

The first first was Peter going public with his belief that Jesus is God. Surrounded by all the pagan gods, Peter proclaimed: "*You are the Christ, the Son of the living God.*" (Matthew 16:16 NIV).

The second huge first was Jesus, declaring His destiny with death: "*Then Jesus made it clear to His disciples that it was now necessary for Him to go to Jerusalem, submit to an ordeal of suffering at the hands of the religious leaders, be killed, and then on the third day be raised alive.*" (Matthew 16:21 MSG)

Third, for the very first time Jesus clarifies that His cross is to be shared by all who follow Him. "*Jesus said to His disciples, 'If any of you wants to be My follower, you must give up your own way, TAKE UP YOUR CROSS and follow Me'*" (Matthew 16:24 NLT)

The flashback fades. When we zoom in on scene three of the day Jesus died, we see an angry wave of hateful humanity streaming through the narrow streets of Jerusalem. In fact, the murderous mob would drive Jesus up the longest, steepest path out of the city. In front with Jesus, as He bore His own instrument of death, would be the Roman soldiers, His executioners. Jesus has already suffered a horrific loss of blood. He gets too weak to bear His bloody burden. Thus, "*As they led Him away, they seized Simon from Cyrene...and put the cross on him and made him carry it behind Jesus.*" (Luke 23:26 NIV)

Neither the Roman soldiers nor the rabble of religious leaders were about to touch the cross of Christ. A cross was considered cursed by God. Whoever touched a cross was touched by the curse. When a physically depleted Jesus fell under the weight of the wood, people jumped back from the cross, like it was a writhing, venomous snake.

They all knew the ancient warning: *"Anyone, who is hung on a tree (cross) is cursed in the sight of God."* (Deuteronomy 21:23 NLT)

Simon was the first person to experience the all-new, redeemed reality: *"Christ redeemed us from the curse...becoming a curse for us."* (Galatians 3:13 NIV)

In that day, it was thought that if one was cursed, he was cut off from the life-giving, loving presence of God. Bearing the curse of our sin, from the cross Jesus cried out: *"My God, My God, why have You forsaken Me?"* (Matthew 27:46 NIV)

Our Lord willingly allowed Himself to be temporarily, yet severely, severed from God's presence. By His full, effective work on the cross we now have eternal, intimate access to ultimate closeness with our God. *"We have confidence to enter the Most Holy Place by the blood of Jesus, by a new and living way opened for us through the curtain, that is His body...Let us draw near to God..."* (Hebrews 10:19,20,22 NIV)

Simon is seemingly, randomly pulled out of the crowd of gawkers to carry the cross for Jesus the rest of the way to the place of brutal, public execution. But what if this is the sovereign hand of a great God doing something big in Simon's one and only life?

Interestingly, no soldier is called by name; no religious leader is named; no bystander is given personal reference.

Only Simon is identified in the most personal way. We know his name. We know his hometown is Cyrene. We know the names of his sons, Alexander and Rufus (Mark 15:21). Simon is mentioned by name by Matthew, Mark and Luke. Most important, Simon is known by Jesus, the Good Shepherd, *"He calls His own sheep by name and leads them..."* (John 10:3 NIV)

Something goes off in me as I study this third scene. I am so keenly aware of my sin. I know I deserve to go to hell for all the lies, for every hurtful word I've said, the hateful deeds done, for all the good I neglected to do. I know the costly price Jesus pays for my salvation. So when I think of Him down in the dirt, gasping, lying in His own blood shed for me, I want to do what Simon did. I want to help Jesus as He suffers for me.

Simon becomes the last person to help Jesus in His human weakness. This moment changed Simon's life forever. It changed his family. His sons, Rufus and Alexander, became leaders in the church. He became a prominent figure in the church. This humble act of service set Jesus free to do something big in his life.

I know I cannot crawl under the cross with Christ. But I can serve Him. I can serve others in His name. I can be His desperado in reckless pursuit of His relentless love. I know: When we serve, we set Jesus up to do something big in our lives!

THE DESPERADO DAILY

Ponder:

"Jesus said to His disciples, 'If any of you wants to be My follower, you must give up your own way, take up your cross, and follow Me.'" (Matthew 16:24 NLT)

Practice:

As Jesus has served you relentlessly, make your life all about serving Jesus.

Pray:

"Lord Jesus, You redeemed me from the curse of my sin. You allowed Your body to be shredded by human vengeance and violence, making a way for me to have intimate, immediate, eternal access to the Heavenly Father. You did not do this for some anonymous somebody. You gave Your life for me. You know me by name. You call me by name. My life is all about serving You. In Your name, Amen."

DESPERADO

DAY 36

A Conversation Between Christ and a Criminal

SCENE FOUR IS madness. The only innocent One who ever lived is having spikes nailed through His wrists and ankles into a rugged timber. Jesus knew no sin and did no sin. Yet nerves are screaming with electric fury up His calves and thighs, across His arms and neck. A shoulder is dislocated. An elbow is wrenched out of joint — all for our sin.

Scene four is utter, appalling humiliation. Jesus is stripped naked. His body loses control of its most basic functions. Some witnesses want to turn away, cover their mouths and noses. Scene four is an ugly, angry assault on the senses, a foul, violent sensory-overload. Out of control, grieving women, beat their breasts. They weep, wailing with ear-piercing shrieks. Scene four is a cacophony of chaos and confusion. The victims, subjected to this agonizing, slow execution, erupt with heart-stopping, blood-curdling screams. The religious spit on the dying body of Jesus, uttering the most vile of insults. The soldiers go about their work with precise, ice-cold. cruel proficiency, taking time to mock, taunt, demean, dishonor, disrespect. It's as gross as it gets.

In scene four Jesus looks like a horror-flick freak. His beard has been forcibly pulled out by the roots. His face, beaten beyond recognition, feels like it's on fire, throbbing with pulsating, searing pain. His whole body has been made into a seeping, bleeding open sore. Flies and gnats attack His flayed flesh.

Scene four is so unjust, so wrong, so sad, so broken, the universe stops working. *"It was now about noon, and darkness came over the whole land until three in the afternoon, for the sun stopped shining."* (Luke 23:44 NIV)

But just before the sun goes out on everything, there's a compelling conversation.

> *"Two other men, both criminals, were also led out with Him to be executed. When they came to the place called the Skull, there they crucified Him along with the criminals — one on His right, the other on His left....One of the criminals, who hung there, hurled insults at Him, 'Aren't You the Christ? Save yourself and us.' But the other criminal rebuked him, 'Don't you fear God, since you are under the same sentence? We are punished justly, for we are getting what our deeds deserve. But this man has done nothing wrong.' Then he said, 'Jesus, remember me when You come into Your Kingdom.' Jesus answered him, 'I tell you the truth, TODAY you will be with Me in paradise'"* (Luke 23:32,33;39-43 NIV)

We can read this seven sentence conversation in a matter of seconds. But to Jesus and the two thieves, it had to feel like it was taking forever. To be crucified was to die of terrifying suffocation. Crucifixion was hideously designed to make death as slow and as unbearably painful as possible. An iron spike was driven through the arches of the feet, but allowing the knees to be flexed. The victim was held spread-eagle to the cross with a spike piercing each wrist, but allowing movement for the arms. Breathing was a complicated, excruciating process. In order to take a breath the victim had to allow all his weight to sag onto the nail impaling his wounded feet. He then had to pull himself up by his tortured wrists to exhale. Having the breath to speak even a few words would be an exercise in the utmost agony.

It must have required the first thief four brutal breaths — four times up and down to spit out his angry attack on Jesus: *"Aren't You...the Christ...save Yourself...and us."* But his raspy railing receives no response from the Savior, who would love to do something big in the first thief's last moments of life.

Then something utterly amazing occurs. I think it is Someone absolutely supernatural. The second thief somehow gets out a total of thirty-nine words. The first thief could only speak eight. The second thief has to go through the same painful process, but it's like he's not going to stop his tortured talking until he hears from Jesus.

It makes me wonder if miraculous mercy is poured out by a caring, compassionate God. Does the second thief receive some kind of special strength in order to humbly confess his sin? Is his pain dramatically diminished, so he can use his last precious breaths to admit his desperate need for a Savior?

It makes me think the heart of God is deeply moved by any sinner desperate enough to call on the name of Jesus. It makes me think that a Sovereign decides how many breaths we get to breathe. It makes me think that a gracious God intervenes in inhales and exhales, when we are using our every breath to recklessly pursue Jesus.

As for Jesus, He doesn't blink an eye. He's enduring the same savage suffering. But this is exactly why He's on the cross. Jesus sighs over that thief's soul the words every desperado longs to hear, *"I tell you the truth, TODAY you will be WITH ME in paradise."*

Notice what it takes for Jesus to do something mercifully and miraculously big in someone's life. The saved thief confessed his own sinful imperfection. He admitted his need for a perfect Savior. He called on the name of Jesus.

Imagine that thief hours later. When his eyes close in death, they instantaneously open in the presence of Jesus. I don't want to think about what happens to the first thief.

It's intriguing to me that only Luke shares this part of the story with us. If you have forgotten, Luke has written this entire account concerning Jesus for one friend, Theophilus. If Luke could have any dream come true, it would be for Jesus to do something big in the life of his friend. I think that's why Luke includes this intimate conversation between a criminal and Christ. Also, when Luke writes his second book for Theophilus, he finds it essential to quote Peter word for word:

"Everyone who calls on the name of the Lord will be saved!" (Acts 2:21 NIV)

THE DESPERADO DAILY

Ponder:

"Everyone who calls on the name of the Lord will be saved!" (Acts 2:21 NIV)

Practice:

Whatever challenge you're facing right now, confess your sin; admit your need for God; call on the name of Jesus!

Pray:

"Dear Lord, I humbly call on Your saving name. With every breath I want to praise You, Jesus. I am forever in Your debt. Your compassion saw me in my need. Your mercy changed the trajectory of my life. Your grace has set me free. As long as you keep me inhaling and exhaling, it is my joy to serve You. In Your name, Amen."

DESPERADO
DAY 37

The Evidence of Being Found

LIFE IS ALL about the hunt. Sometimes we get life backwards, thinking we must be on the hunt. We think our happiness depends on hunting for the right person to love, hunting for the right place to live, hunting for the right job and the right amount of money, hunting for the right pile of possessions. We hunt, hunt, hunt, but never hunt down happiness.

What if we are not made to hunt? What if we are designed to be hunted? What if that is why you are reading this book right now? What if true happiness only happens when you are found? Jesus, the Lord of life, is on the hunt for you!

Here's a tremendous spiritual reality to let tickle around in your mind. For some time now Jesus has been stalking you like a shadow. He is relentless. It's a day by day thing. Jesus got you out of bed today, so you could be found by Him.

Truth be told, Jesus wants you more than found. He wants you full — full of joy, full of hope, full of peace, full of blessing, full of abundance. He wants you more than found and full. Jesus wants you free — free of all guilt and shame, free of fear and worry, free of anxiety and depression, free of anything that painfully limits your life, free to be His best version of you. Jesus wants you found, because He has plans to make you come alive!

Maybe you want to say with a bit of sarcasm, "The last time I checked I am alive." Let me ask you: has this thought ever crossed your mind? "Isn't there more to life than this?" In a moment of inner honesty have you ever said, "I love my family. I'm grateful for my job. I have friends. But I can feel so empty. Isn't there more to life than this?"

Do you think that question just comes out of your own mind? What if it's Jesus testing your soul with a pop quiz, "Isn't there more to life than this?" What if inner emptiness is evidence that Jesus is on the hunt for you. He wants you found, full and free!

I want to illustrate this by introducing you to the prototype of a person who gets found by Jesus. This guy is super successful. He is driven to be the best in his field. He is a passionate visionary who will stop at nothing to make his dreams come true. He will let no one stand in his way. He is a man on a mission. But none of that has anything to do with why Jesus wants to hunt him down until he knows he is found.

What makes this man so credible for our purposes is that he hates the very name of Jesus. He does not believe that Jesus was God come to earth in human flesh. He certainly does not believe that Jesus rose from the dead. He's glad Jesus is dead. He has no idea what happened to the body of Jesus. But that's secondary. It does not matter. The only thing that matters is stopping the incredible momentum of this massive Jesus movement. All he cares about is killing anyone and everyone who claims to be a follower of Jesus.

That's when he walks right into a brilliant, blinding flash of light, when out of nowhere Jesus appears in all His glory. It blinds this guy. He's down on his hands and knees. A Voice pins him in place, "Saul, Saul, why are you out to get Me?" (Acts 9:4 MSG)

Saul whispers, "Who is this?" The Voice thunders, "You know who this is. I am Jesus. Get up now and get into town. I'll let you know what I want you to do next."

When Saul gets up, he's still blind. He stays blind for three days. By the way, how many days was Jesus in the tomb? What do you think goes on in Saul's mind for those three days? It's the same thing that goes on in our minds when we come face-to-face with this fact: we've been living our lives in the wrong direction, away from God.

It is another indication that Jesus wants you found, when *you can't rid your mind of all your regret.* You wish you could go back in time. If you could only undo some hurtful things you've done, take back some hateful words you've said, if you could just get a do-over. You can make yourself so sick with regret, it's hard to eat or sleep.

But if Jesus is anything, He is compassionate. He only leaves you in your regret long enough so that you want to be found. This is the turning point of your life, when you are ready to surrender everything to Jesus. *This is the whole hope of the holy hunt — that you will surrender your life fully to Jesus!*

Here's how it happened for Saul. Just as Jesus got you into this book today, so He got someone to Saul to deliver this unmistakable message. "What are you waiting for? Get up and get yourself baptized, scrubbed clean of those sins and personally acquainted with God!" (Acts 22:16 MSG)

Evidently for the past three days the resurrected Jesus had been speaking to Saul. "Be baptized. Let Me fill your inner emptiness with Myself. I want to forgive all your sins. Let me cleanse you of all guilt and shame. I want you found, full and free."

Saul did not need to be told twice. "Immediately something like scales fell from Saul's eyes, and he could see again. He got up and was baptized." (Acts 9:18 NIV)

From this point forward no one wrote down more about Jesus' resurrection and our baptism than this man, who became known as the Apostle Paul. Here are examples.

Paul writes: "This is what baptism into the life of Jesus means. When we are lowered into the water, it is like the burial of Jesus; when we are raised up out of the water, it is like the resurrection of Jesus." (Romans 6:3,4 MSG)

"If we have been united with Jesus in a death like His (in baptism), we will certainly also be united with Him in a resurrection like His." (Romans 6:5 NIV)

"Having been buried with Christ in baptism, in which you were also raised with Him through your faith in the working of God, who raised Christ from the dead." (Colossians 2:12 NIV)

Inspired by God, the Apostle Paul makes a big deal of Jesus' resurrection and our baptism. So, Jesus' resurrection and baptism is a big deal to all desperados. In our passionate pursuit of Jesus, we are desperate to experience Him fully by sharing with Him in His death, burial and resurrection through baptism. Our baptism is evidence of our being found by Jesus.

THE DESPERADO DAILY

Ponder:

"If we have been united with Jesus in a death like His (in baptism), we will certainly also be united with Him in a resurrection like His." (Romans 6:5 NIV)

Practice:

Thank Jesus for stalking you like a shadow to find you, fill you and free you.

Pray:

"Dear Lord, I want to be found by You. I want to be filled with Your zest for life, Your peace, patience and joy. Free me, please, to love myself and be kind to others. Free me to love You with all my heart. Free me to know You. In Your name, Amen."

DESPERADO

DAY 38

His Word

A HALF DOZEN times I have been to Israel with groups of people from our church. We're not on vacation. I don't consider it a tour. It's more a spiritual pilgrimage. We want to walk where Jesus walked, see the holy sites as they were seen by Jesus.

There are highlights all along the way — baptisms in the Jordan River, sailing on the Sea of Galilee, visiting Bethlehem, the birthplace of Christ. But one special place is always saved until last as a fitting, closing climax to each trip.

You might think it would be the walk up the Via Dolorosa. This "way of suffering" is thought to be the route taken by Jesus as He carried His cross. This narrow street ends at the Church of the Holy Sepulcher, which commemorates the place where Jesus was crucified and buried. But on some trips to Israel we have skipped a visit to this church. It's a struggle to believe it marks the actual place of Christ's crucifixion and resurrection because it is inside the old city walls. In the day of Jesus, crucifixions and burials were done outside the city.

Though I love to walk the Via Dolorosa, it seems more consistent with Scripture for it to end outside the old city. That's where we go for the most memorable experience on each trip to the Holy Land. Modern archeology has unearthed two important finds — a cliff face, bearing the image of a human skull and a garden tomb.

Jesus was crucified at Calvary, the skull. Jesus was buried near Calvary in a garden tomb (John 19:41). This tomb is cut into the face of a rock, as was the tomb of Jesus. This was obviously a wealthy person's tomb. A rich man, Joseph of Arimathea, buried Jesus in his own personal tomb. At the base of this garden tomb is a trough, where a stone could be rolled across the entrance, like the tomb of Jesus.

If this garden tomb is not the exact one used by Jesus from late afternoon Friday until early Sunday morning, it sure feels like it. When we're there, we each by turn enter the tomb for quiet moments of reflection. Then as a group we gather to share communion.

This is not meant to be a travelogue. You may never visit the Garden Tomb outside the old city of Jerusalem. But this is the beauty and power of God's inspired Word. It does not cost a dime and you can visit the crucifixion and resurrection of Jesus anytime you want (Matthew 27:27-28:10; Mark 15:16-16:16; Luke 23:26-24:12; John 19:17-20:23).

It's not about being in a special place or if a certain place is authentic. It's about faith.

So, before I take you into Luke's account of the empty tomb, let's take one last look at that blood-stained cross. I just want to camp a minute on two facts. First, "When Jesus had cried out again in a loud voice, He GAVE up His spirit." (Matthew 27:50 NIV)

It's important to realize that Jesus was not murdered. He willingly gave His life for you on the cruel cross. Jesus had made this fact undeniably clear. "I freely lay down My life.... No one takes it from Me, I lay it down of My own free will." (John 10:17,18)

When Jesus died on the cross, He was giving His life for you to pay for your sins. That is the centerpiece of all Scripture. "Christ died for our sins, according to the Scriptures.... He was buried.... He was raised on the third day according to the Scriptures." (I Corinthians 15:3,4 NIV)

Died. Buried. The buried part is huge, because this means Jesus was fully physically dead. He was not merely wounded and unconscious so He could somehow recover.

Here's the account of an eyewitness to the crucifixion. "The soldiers...came to Jesus and found that He was already dead.... One of the soldiers pierced Jesus' side with a spear, bringing a sudden flow of blood and water." (John 19:33,34)

Irrefutable physical evidence that Jesus absolutely died. Buried. "Joseph...took down the body, wrapped it in linen, and placed it in a tomb cut out of rock. Then he rolled a stone against the entrance of the tomb." (Mark 15:46 NIV)

Died 3:00 p.m. Friday. Buried 6:00 p.m. Friday. Friday night is a sleepless night for the followers of Jesus. Saturday is 24 hours of constant, unrelenting grief, anxiety and fear and then another agonizing, sleepless night. Now let's take up the resurrection story.

"At the crack of dawn on Sunday, the women came to the tomb carrying the burial spices they had prepared. They found the entrance stone rolled back from the tomb, so they walked in. But once inside, they could not find the body of the Master, Jesus. They were puzzled, wondering what to make of it. Then out of nowhere it seemed, two men, light cascading over them, stood there. The women were awestruck and bowed down in worship. The men said, 'Why are you looking for the Living One in a cemetery? He is not here. He is risen. Remember how He told you...that He had to be handed over to sinners, be killed on a cross, and in three days rise up? Then they remembered Jesus' words." (Luke 24:1-8)

I find this fascinating. This is the very first Easter. Jesus has done the unbelievable, the unprecedented and the absolute impossible. Jesus has risen from the dead. But when these women show up as potential witnesses, He is nowhere to be found.

What's up with that? You'd think Jesus would be all full of Himself and doing a dance outside that empty tomb. It's like Jesus is playing hide-and-seek with these women.

Can you relate? Do you ever feel like Jesus is playing hide-and-seek with you? You're a mess. You're confused. You don't know where to turn. You decide to turn to Jesus, but it feels like you come up empty. You think, "Maybe I'm not doing it right." You think, "Maybe I'm not good enough." What do you do when it feels like Jesus does not want to be found? You do what the women did. "Then they remembered Jesus' words!"

I know it was more spectacular than that. Dazzling, snow-white angels show up. Why doesn't Jesus show up in person? Why does He just send a couple of assistants?

Angels are messengers. These angels are delivering a message for Jesus because the women did not have what we have. We have all the words of Jesus — the Bible.

If Jesus had been there in person to greet the women, "Hey, check it out, ladies. See who I am. See what I did. You know I'm God," from that point forward those women would base their relationship with Jesus on sensational experience. "If we're not having some kind of sensational experience, we must not be finding Jesus."

Nothing could be further from the truth. Jesus wants to be found in His Word. Jesus wants to be known by His Word. Jesus wants to relate to us through His Word. When you're a mess and you're looking for Jesus, look in His Word. In fact, maybe our lives won't become a mess if we make a practice of meeting Jesus in His Word.

Here's the desperado take-away. Jesus wants us to trust and obey His Word!

THE DESPERADO DAILY

Ponder:

"Then they remembered His words" (Luke 24:8 NIV).
"I have told you these things so that you will be filled
with My joy" (John 15:11 NLT). "Heaven and earth
will pass away, but My words will never pass away"
(Matthew 24:35 NIV)

Practice:

Trust and obey the words of Jesus.

Pray:

*"Dear Jesus, my heart agrees with the heart of Peter,
when he said, 'Lord, to whom shall we go? You have the
words of eternal life. We believe and know that You are
the Holy One of God!" Holy Spirit, please, motivate me
to read the Word regularly, to meditate on the Word and
to remember the words of Jesus. In His name, Amen."*

DESPERADO

DAY 39

A Perfect Peace

JESUS IS ABOUT to play another game of hide-and-seek — this time with men.

Whoa. Now wait a minute. When I say that Jesus is playing hide-and-seek, I am in no way suggesting that Jesus likes to play games with us or that He ever plays games with anyone. It's just a figure of speech. I'm simply having a little fun with words. Okay, I'll be dead serious. Jesus is NOT into games. Jesus is completely into growth. This is very personal. Jesus is completely into your growth in your relationship with Him.

We are about to see that Jesus works differently in different people's lives, based on what helps each person grow. Jesus did not interact in the very same way with Peter, John, Zacchaeus, Paul or with you and me. He works in each person's life in whatever way is necessary to promote (and sometimes provoke) the most growth.

Earlier on that first Easter morning, Jesus refrained from giving the women a sensational experience of Himself. He would later greet them in person and allow them to touch the wounds in His wrists and side. But with

Jesus, it's first things first. The highest priority for on-going growth in a relationship with Him is a focus on His Word.

The sensational is insubstantial to sustain any relationship that is to become enduring and endearing. Many people get their miracles and still drift away from a good God. Or people get mad because they shout, "Jump," and Jesus does not say, "How high?"

I believe in miracles. I believe there are times when Jesus chooses to do wonders in our lives. But He is God. It's His choice. He chooses what most helps us grow.

Whew! I'm glad I got that off my chest. Let's get back to our story.

Jesus is about to play another game of hide and seek — this time with men who are going in the wrong direction. "That same day two of them were going to a village called Emmaus, about seven miles from Jerusalem." (Luke 24:13 NIV)

What the heck! These men are going away from Jesus. The cross is in Jerusalem. The work of Jesus is in Jerusalem. The empty tomb is in Jerusalem. The victory of Jesus is in Jerusalem. These guys are going in the wrong direction away from Jesus. What happens to someone who chooses to move away from Jesus?

"They were talking with each other about everything that had happened. As they talked and discussed these things with each other, Jesus Himself came up and walked along with them; but they were kept from recognizing Him." (Luke 24:14-16)

I love this. Do you see what's happening here? When these men make a move away from Jesus, He hunts them down. The same is true of us. The cross is irrefutable evidence that Jesus will go to any length to get to us and turn us around when we're going away from Him. But He will often do it by playing hide-and-seek.

Jesus keeps these guys from recognizing Him. Why didn't He just jump out from behind a bush and yell, "It's Me — alive and kicking, baby"? They might run all the way back to Jerusalem and tell everybody. But Jesus does what will best grow stronger faith.

Notice how Jesus engages them. This is important, because He has you reading this today to engage you. "He asked them, 'What are you discussing together as you walk along?' They stood still, their faces downcast." (Luke 24:17 NIV)

Moving away from Jesus drives us in only one way — the direction of the downcast.

Here's what got them going in the wrong direction. Here's what will get us downcast. "One of them...asked Him, 'Are you only a visitor to Jerusalem and do not know the things that have happened there in these days?' 'What things?' Jesus asked. 'About Jesus of Nazareth,' they replied, "He was a prophet, powerful in word and deed before God and all the people.'" (Luke 24:18,19 NIV)

No wonder they were downcast. They only saw Jesus as a man, a religious man, a prophet, but nothing more. Whenever you see Jesus as less than God, downcast is the only direction your life can take.

But it gets worse for these wrong-direction guys. They continue, "Our rulers handed Jesus over to be sentenced to death, and they crucified Him. But we HAD HOPED He was the One!" (Luke 24:20,21 NIV)

A life where Jesus is not the One to rescue, deliver and save, puts hope in the past tense. It becomes a hopeless life. But remember, Jesus relentlessly hunts us down to restore our hope and make our relationship with Him come alive.

Jesus laid it out straight. *"You are such foolish, foolish people! You find it so hard to believe all...the Scriptures. Wasn't it clearly predicted by the prophets that the Messiah would have to suffer all these things before entering His time of glory?' Then Jesus quoted them passage after passage...beginning with Genesis and going right through the Scriptures, explaining what the passages meant and what they said about Himself."* (Luke 24:25-27 LB)

I've heard it said and I love to say it: Everything in the Bible means something and everything points to Jesus! The Bible is the Word of Jesus and it's all about Him.

If I can cut to the chase, these guys did come to recognize Jesus, as He revealed Himself, after taking them through the truth of Scripture. They returned to Jerusalem and met with the other followers of Jesus

Now Jesus has all His followers right where He wants them, just like He has you right here, where He wants you. Are you ready for a deeply personal, profound experience of Jesus? That's what He gave them. *"Jesus appeared to them and said, 'Peace be with you!'"* (Luke 24:36 MSG)

This word for "peace" is a strong word. It speaks of fullness. It is the only antidote to your gnawing, inner emptiness. This peace, which only Jesus gives, fills you with joy unspeakable, love unlimited and an indestructible hope. This is the peace desperados find in their reckless pursuit of Jesus as He reveals Himself through His Word.

But this peace is more. This peace speaks of getting free — free of old emotional aches, old hurtful habits and old, ugly issues; free of all guilt and shame; free to live out God's dream for your life.

This peace is all about the supernatural power of God at work in your life. A perfect peace, based on the same incomparably great power that raised Jesus from the dead.

Here's what the written Word promises of Jesus, the living Word: *"You will keep in perfect peace all who trust in You, all whose thoughts are fixed on You!"* (Isaiah 26:3 NLT)

THE DESPERADO DAILY

THE DESPERADO DAILY

Ponder:

> "You will keep in perfect peace all who trust in You, all whose thoughts are fixed on You!" (Isaiah 26:3 NLT)

Practice:

> When you read the written Word, expect Jesus, the living Word, to be revealed.

Pray:

> *"Dear Lord, I know I have been as foolish and slow to believe all the Scriptures as those men on the road to Emmaus. Please forgive me. And please help me. Every time I go into Your Word, speak to me. Reveal Yourself to me. I am in reckless pursuit of Your relentless love. I want my trust in You based on Your Word. In Your name, Amen."*

DESPERADO
DAY 40

Sent to Serve

I AM SO excited for us to be in this moment together right now. The Lord has given me something very specific to share with you. What He told me I'm telling you. This is what He put on my heart for you. YOU HAVE NO IDEA WHAT YOU'VE DONE!

This is it. This is day 40. For the past 39 days, you've been doing reckless pursuit of your relentless Jesus. He keeps inviting you into this book, into His presence, into His Word and you keep saying, "Yes, yes, yes!" When you say, "yes" to Jesus, you say "yes" to an exciting, epic banquet of blessings and promises.

Life will always be hard and hurtful. But when you're a desperado recklessly saying "yes" to Jesus, He gets you through all the trauma and trouble. He gets you all the way to triumph. Thankfully, you worship with the psalmist: "O my soul, bless God. From head to toe, I'll bless His holy name! O my soul, bless God, don't forget a single blessing! He forgives your sins — every one. He heals your diseases — every one. He redeems you from hell — saves your life. He crowns you with love and mercy —

a paradise crown. He wraps you in goodness — beauty eternal. He renews your youth — you're always young in His presence. God makes everything come out right; He puts victims back on their feet." (Psalm 103:1-6 MSG)

God gets us back on our feet with everything coming out right. With the desperado psalmist we sing to God: "You are holy, enthroned on the praises..." (Psalm 22:3)

I love the way the Japanese Bible renders this verse. "When we worship, we build a big chair (throne) for God to sit in!" (Psalm 22:3 Japanese Bible)

Desperados, look what you do when you worship. Your praise puts you so close to the throne of God, you can hear the Word of Christ. This is extraordinary good news because: "Faith comes by hearing...the Word of Christ." (Romans 10:17 NIV)

This makes desperados want to draw even closer to the Lord of life. "Let us then approach God's throne of grace with confidence, so that we may receive mercy and find grace to help us in our time of need." (Hebrews 4:16 NIV)

Being served well by our good God makes us want to serve our good God well. "If any of you wants to serve Me, then follow Me. Then you'll be where I am, ready to serve at a moment's notice. The Father will honor and reward anyone who serves Me." (John 12:26 MSG). This is not the only reason desperados stay in reckless pursuit of Jesus. It's not the main reason. But it's a good reason. God is a relentless rewarder of those who serve.

This new desperado life of reckless worship, reckless service and relentless reward begins as we follow Jesus in baptism. "We were therefore buried with Him through baptism into death in order that, just as Christ was raised from the dead through the glory of the Father, we too may live a new (desperado) life!" (Romans 6:4 NIV)

That concise summary of the desperado life is illustrated beautifully in one of my favorite Jesus stories. Only Luke records this account. He does it solely for his friend, Theophilus. But now, 2,000 years later, we are the blessed beneficiaries.

"One Sabbath, when Jesus went to eat in the house of a prominent Pharisee, He was being carefully watched. There in front of Him was a man suffering from abnormal swelling of his body. Jesus asked the Pharisee and the experts of the law, 'Is it lawful to heal on the Sabbath or not?' But they remained silent. So taking hold of the man, He healed him and sent him on his way." (Luke 14:1-4)

Luke does not waste words. It's a very brief account, only a handful of sentences. But evidently Luke saw this scene as essential to understanding Jesus, the divine desperado. I see it as having incredible supernatural implications. I pray it every day for someone.

Let's slip into this scenario with Jesus. At the entrance of a luxurious home, there is a sign that reads: "No desperados allowed!" Jesus enters anyway. This is huge. The house belongs to a rich religious nazi who would love to see Jesus dead. This is not an act of courage by Jesus. This is an open display of His unconditional acceptance. Jesus will enter wherever He is invited.

This moves me at the deepest level. It means Jesus will enter my life — every aspect of my life — if I invite Him. My life is at best deeply flawed and at worst filthy with sin. But nothing stops our Jesus from accepting a desperate invitation. How can we not pursue such a relentlessly gracious Jesus who promised: *"Here I am! I stand at the door and knock. If ANYONE hears My voice and opens the door, I will come in and eat with him, and he with Me."* (Revelation 3:20 NIV)

This dinner happens on the Sabbath, the Jewish day of worship. Everyone and anyone gets into God's House. So after worship, the wealthy take turns hosting an exclusive, social event — a big dinner with no riff-raff allowed. Jesus is invited by the really religious guy like a spider invites a fly into a web. It's a trap. Jesus "was being carefully watched."

Here was the trap. Directly across the table from Jesus "was a man suffering from abnormal swelling of the body."

This was an incredibly painful physical condition. The man's body was bloated beyond belief. He likely could not walk or feed himself or clean himself or take care of himself.

Some group of someones had obviously carried him to this spot to be within touching distance of Jesus. You see, on the Sabbath it was the religious law to be chill. But Jesus lived by a higher, irreligious standard: be compassionate whatever day of the week it is. Jesus would break the religious law to help a person in desperate need.

Jesus springs a trap of His own, when He challenges the religious holier-than-thous: "Is it lawful to heal on the Sabbath or not?" They choke on their self-righteous arrogance.

I think Jesus smiles and takes their silence as a big "Yes!" It's not like He's looking for their permission anyway. Jesus always takes action based on His relentless love. But what He does no one sees coming.

When Luke writes, *"taking hold of the man, He healed him",* he uses a very, very strong Greek verb ("epilabano"), which means "to physically, forcibly seize."

In my mind's eye, I see Jesus getting up from the table and striding quickly over to the disabled man. Jesus leans down and physically, forcibly seizes the man, lifting him and cradling him in His arms. Jesus holds the helpless man tightly, yet tenderly, to His chest. In this holy hug, Jesus heals the man. His painfully bloated body returns to its pain-free normal condition.

This is why I pray this part of the story over people I care deeply about every day. I want to pray them into the strong and safe arms of Jesus. Jesus is full of compassion and loves to show mercy. So, I cry out for Jesus to take hold of them and heal them.

This has been my dream for you over the past 40 days. My highest hope was for you to recklessly pursue your way right into the arms of Jesus. My prayer has been for Him to physically, forcibly seize you; tightly and tenderly hold you; to give you a holy hug with help and hope and healing. I want to pray you into the arms of Jesus. But I also want to pray you out of the arms of our Lord. That's what happened in our story. Jesus healed him "and sent him on his way."

This is how you know you have achieved desperado status. When you recklessly pursue Jesus, He relentlessly serves you.

That's what happened to Isaiah when he found himself in the very presence of the Lord. *"Then I heard the voice of the LORD saying, 'Whom shall I send? Who will go for us?' And I said, 'Here am I. Send me."* (Isaiah 6:8 NIV)

That's the heartcry of every desperado. It's the dream of Jesus for every desperado. He made this clear on the day He conquered death. *"As the Father has sent Me, I am sending you!"* (John 20:21 NIV)

We are sent to bring our community to Jesus and to bring Jesus to our community. We are sent, with an unshakable sense of belonging, to help others know they belong. We are sent to serve in His name and grow in His likeness.

This is the prayer of every desperado: "Here am I. Send me."

THE DESPERADO DAILY

Ponder:

"Then I heard the voice of the LORD saying, 'Whom shall I send? Who will go for us?' And I said, 'Here am I. Send me.'" (Isaiah 6:8 NIV) "As the Father has sent Me, I am sending you!" (John 20:21 NIV)

Practice:

Make a list of friends and family. Consider their concerns. Pray for Jesus to take them up in His arms of compassion, holding them, helping them and healing them.

Pray:

"I bless You, Lord Jesus. All You have ever done is bless me."

With Gratitude

To my son, Joshua, who is always willing to help his dad. I'll never be smart or talented like Josh; but I love working with him. He makes everything better and more fun.

To my friend and co-laborer for His sake, Robin Benskin, who in addition to being our awesome office manager, graciously edited all my work. It's always good to have a friend smarter than yourself.

To my daughter-in-law, Marissa, who is technically strong where I am weak. I would be a mess without her organizational and computer skills.

To my friend, Amanda Urish, who didn't hesitate in her willingness to help me. I respect her skills as a graphic artist. I am grateful for her commitment to always do her best. But most of all, I love her heart for Jesus and her humility in serving Him.

Made in the USA
Lexington, KY
04 September 2017